Magdalena Augustyniak, 1956-

"The Eternal Love", a true story of psychological nature/ by Magdalena Augustyniak. One with compassion will find a healing power in it

Continuation Series of "The Journey"

Previous Series:

"Our Journey to the Better World"
ISBN-13:
978-1516962549

ISBN-10:
1516962540

And its Polish Translation:

"Nasza Podróż Do Lepszego Świata"
Library of Congress Control Number: 2016907398
ISBN-13:
978-1532984556

ISBN-10:
1532984553

Both published by CreateSpace Independent Publishing Platform, North Charleston, SC and available on Amazon.com

Description

"The Eternal Love", Series #2 of "The Journey" is a true story, dealing with social psychology of 21st century. In the midst of daily experiences, legends, myths, and religious beliefs are hidden many morals. The book truly portrays the agony of one's decades-long psychological suffering. That suffering, attributed to continued 'civilization' or modernization of today's world, is inflicted by electronic channels and carried out by people with no scruples, people completely stripped of a human face. It may raise a question, where are we heading to? Will this civilization vanish, too, like many before? Or will the 21st century man at last wake up and realize that only one chance does he get in that human body he assumed at birth!

About the Author

Magdalena Augustyniak was born on 02/24/1956 in Nowy Sącz, Poland to Jan Eugeniusz and Władyslawa Kocemba, residing in the village of Kamionka Wielka. She is the sister of six siblings, four sisters: Marta Morańska, Maria Górska, Matylda Ziemborak, and Monika Pazgan; as well as two brothers: Marek Kocemba and Maciej Kocemba. Magdalena graduated with honors from Grammar School #1 in Kamionka Wielka in 1971 and went to High School, II Liceum Ogólnokształcące Imieniem Marii Konopnickiej in Nowy Sącz. She majored in Math and Physics. She was a very good student, and excelled in both, Polish language and Math. In her life she must have read at least a hundred of books and most of them belonged to her grandfather, Józef. She found them on his attic. He was always her idol. She was broken-hearted, then, when he passed away on 02/29/1972 at the age of 86. Shortly after, on 07/03/1973 she lost her grandmother, Stefania Kocemba to whom she was very close too. From her youngest years, she had a difficulty dealing with the concept of death, so her father's death on 09/04/1982 was the biggest blow yet. Her maternal grandfather, Franciszek Ptak she never even knew because he died when her mother was only 15 years of age. He left his wife, Katarzyna Ptak with 10 children. Magdalena could never forget her mother's stories how she and her siblings were always starving. The saddest part of the story was, though, that her grandmother Katarzyna received a lump sum payment after her husband's death and it would have made them rich if it wasn't for the government changing the currency value. Anyway, Magdalena grew up in hardship too but at the same time in the loving family atmosphere. In July of 1974 she came to America to her father's cousin, Mary Augustyniak who sponsored her for a housekeeping job, to help her family. Thanks to one lady, named Jean Palermo who spoke on her behalf to her aunt, she was able to finish her fourth year of High School and graduated from Battin in 1976. In the spring of 1978 she met her husband Jozef Augustyniak who came visiting her Aunt Mary and Uncle Al. She fell in love with him and on 05/27/1979 they got married. On 08/06/1980 their first daughter, Angelica was born and three years later on 10/31/1983, their son, Brandon John. On 12/14/1989 Jessica was born. As of 2016, Magdalena still lives in Elizabeth, NJ and has two grandchildren too, Alexander and Anastasia Vazquez, Angelica's children, 20 and 18 years of age.

The Eternal Love

By

Magdalena Augustyniak
Maiden Name: Kocemba

Dedicated to three children: Angelica, Brandon, and Jessica Augustyniak
And two grandchildren: Alexander and Anastasia Vazquez
And all my Family in Poland, especially to my mother.

And in loving memory of Zbigniew Wroblewski, my cousin who was like a brother to me and who
allegedly was killed in Germany and expired on December 31, 2016

There is a place on this Earth called Kamionka Wielka. It is such a wondrous village. Once there were no wars there, no jealousy, no greed, or slyness. Couples did not have to fear for their relationships to be broken up, since all men and women looked the same. They were all beautiful, and their souls were clean like God's angels. There were no lonely men or women, for everyone had someone to love. Men appreciated their partners, women. They nurtured them, especially when they were carrying their children in the womb. Every woman expecting a child had special privileges. She was being treated like a queen and everywhere she went, she received a warm welcome. Expecting woman was loved by her spouse, more than ever. There was nothing that he would not do for her. Children were considered God's most precious gift. They grew up content, confident, and strong in the loving family atmosphere. They enjoyed playing with each other and taking part in festivities that took place on the seventh day of each week. That was the time to give praise to God for his kindness and guardianship, as well as to celebrate the unity and love of the community.

That place was once a home to the greatest man on Earth that Ada ever knew. It was her grandfather. His name was Jozef. During the 1st World War he was in the Austrian Army because that part of Poland was then under the occupation of that country. During the fight on the Russian territory, he was captured and imprisoned in Russia but survived even the October 1917 Revolution of which he had many tales to tell later on, to the school children that came to visit. He was also compelled to tell them about the legendary Paradise the village was once blessed with. It seemed so wonderful. Nature was kind to humans since they learned to respect it. They needed not to sweat anymore, as the sun gave just enough of energy, to give men light and warmth. There were no droughts or floods. Rain kept the trees and grass green, kept the flowers blooming, and gave men just as much water as they needed. After each rainfall a magnificent rainbow emerged across the sky. That was the sign from God that he was pleased with what he was seeing. There was no sickness or diseases, no tears shed. All people had natural and other resources that they needed, so men did not need to travel and there was no need for cars. Wild animals kept their distance from men, but were not afraid of them. Boys and girls had common wisdom and knowledge of everything, so the schools were for more of a recreational activity reasons than learning.

Children were curious to find out what happened to that Paradise and he told them it was lost and it was all because of one little girl who ate the red apple from the forbidden tree. She was not being spiteful or disobedient to her father but just had her reasons confused. Her father's face turned white as a sheet when she told him: "Daddy, I found the red apple fallen from the forbidden tree and it was not poisonous at all. In fact, it was delicious." From that day on all bad things began to happen to her family and to the entire village, as if the Evil has found its way in to continue his master work. The youngsters were questioning Jozef if it was possible to bring that world back. Ada's grandfather's eyes filled up with tears, as he was trying to give the answer to those innocent, elementary school children. He did not want to disappoint them, so he said: "Paradise is up to you, my dear children. I believe it is something that can be given by God's grace, to his creation. For this to happen, men have to rid themselves from all the wrongdoing and learn to love unconditionally". Ada's grandfather was pleased to see that the children's faces lighted up. The idea that the future was at their hands and Paradise might be just as real as they were, sounded pretty good to them.

Ada had a different view on the Evil than her grandfather did, though. She blamed it all on the modernization of her village, especially electricity. Yet, electricity seemed like magic to her. She could never comprehend what it was or how it worked. In fact, she was scared of those electric lines on the poles. She heard strange sounds, as she was passing by them every day, to and from school. It seemed to her, as if there was life in them. Was she losing her mind, or were those electric currents really speaking to her, as she thought? Despite of it, she could not overcome the feeling that indeed she did something wrong by eating that red apple fallen from the forbidden tree.

Ada was right. Something wrong had gone for sure, when she ate that apple, but she could no longer strain her memory. She tried to paste some pieces together, but the puzzle did not make any sense. Her Aunt Hel's wedding was part of the puzzle, but all she could remember was carrying the paintings of the Sacred Hearts of Mary and Jesus. Then, it was that one terrifying night. All the neighbors seemed to have gone mad. They were acting wicked and reciting verses that were making her hair stand up. The night was misty and seemed as if something evil was in it. Everyone seemed so strange to her. She was not herself since that day on and thought of that night as "The Spell". Soon, her mother was to bear the fruit of it, Ada's youngest sister, Akin.

Couple years later, Ada's mother had another child yet, but the baby was still born. Ada blamed herself for that. She was told to stay at her grandma Kat' house, when her mother went to give birth. No one explained that to her, though. She kept crying for her mother every day. She was worried that something horrible has happened to her. Finally, the news came, but only to make her even more disturbed. She was told that Ada's mother was in the hospital to give birth to her eighth child. Unfortunately, something went wrong, and, intentionally or not, Ateu was still born. Ada thought it was her fault. If she did not cry for her mother, would her brother have been fine?

As Ada was troubled by the memories of the darkness that overshadowed her village and by the death of her brother, the weather has gone totally bizarre. During the winter the village was completely buried in the snow. One day, as she was going to school in the blizzard, she could not see anything. Her eyes were tearing and her cheeks were burning from the snow. All around her was the total whiteness, and she found herself walking in circles. The snow was so deep that she could hardly move. A few times, she fell into a dune of snow and had trouble digging herself out. Finally, she found her way back home. The whole time she was only a few meters away from it. Springtime and summer that followed the rough winter brought severe floods and thunder storms. Ada was very frightened of thunder and lightning because many times the lightning struck the electrical fuse box in their house. The scariest experience, though, was to get caught in the electrical storm outdoors, with the roaring thunder and the blue flashes of light.

A little sunshine did soon seep through Ada's four walls, though. Her whole body trembled and her heart pounded, every time her cousin Naj came by. She soon discovered that he had feelings for her too. They loved to spend time together. They had so much in common, not that they had much to talk about, but for the most time just walked, holding hands. When they found a good spot in the shade, they would just lie there for hours, holding each other closely. They needed not to say anything, as if their souls were united in one. It was so peaceful around, only they and the birds chirping happily in the trees, and the wonderful scents of wild flowers.

Ada's mother would soon put the end to that little romance. She found Ada and Naj under the tree a few times. She forbade them to go out together. Ada had the feeling that Naj was told to stop coming to her house. After all, Naj was Ada's first cousin and she was supposed to suppress any feelings she may have had towards him. She was heartbroken, as she was waiting every day that he may show up. She did not want to speak to anyone, did not want to eat, and grew very thin. She thought it was unfair to break her relationship, when she and Naj were nothing but the best friends.

It was nighttime, and Ada was clenching her teeth and clutching the ends of the sheet on her bed, to quench the cries from excruciating pain in her lower abdominal area. She felt feverish and surely thought that she was going to die. Her grandmother Stef was putting compresses of hot oats on her abdomen, but she only wanted to scream even more. Was she going to die? Hours and hours passed in that agony, and finally the pain somewhat subsided, and Ada fell asleep. In the morning, she had to go to the bathroom, a little portable shack behind the house. She ran back in the house, babbling that she must be hurt, for she had blood dripping down her legs. Ada's mom told her, though, that there was nothing wrong with her. She explained that she just got her first period. "It is normal," she said, "for all growing girls". There were no pads in those days, so Ada's mom improvised a sort of padding from some old T-shirts. She told her to wash them, when they got soiled. Ada's mother washed clothes by hand, in the buckets, and then hanged them outside on the lines, but Ada would go down the hill, to the creek to wash her personal items. She would soon learn about menstruation at school. Her classmates seemed to have no problem with it at all. Ada, however, was different. Every menstrual period, she suffered terrible migraines and cramps in her lower abdomen that she could hardly bear, and her blood flow was very large. Sometimes she had to leave her grammar school and run back home. But not through the road, no! She could not have people looking at her bloody legs. She ran through the hills and the creeks, until she reached home. She would get washed but, unfortunately, there was nothing in the house to stop her pain; so she would slip under the covers, clench her teeth, and curl up like a little baby.

Ada and her siblings loved their maternal grandmother, Kat. She would share with her grandchildren everything that she had. Even though her house was only roughly finished, Ada always felt warmth in it. The house had only a kitchen and one room. There was no flooring, but just a bare ground. Grandma Kat was not only a great cook and a baker, but also a seamstress. As for cooking and baking, it was only from the weddings that her grandchildren got their fill, but sewing was another thing. Grandma Kat would make new clothes from the old, funny-looking dresses and skirts that sometimes Grandma Stef received in packages, from her sister in America. One time she even got satin material, decorated with delicate flowers. Grandma Kat sewed dresses from it, one for Ada and one for Mar. Ada and Mar were beautiful girls but their bellies always stuck out, as if they were pregnant. Could it be that it was from malnutrition? Ada's mother used to always tell them: "Walk straight and pull your bellies in" but it was easier said than done.

When Ada and her sister, Mar were very young, they used to play that they were married. Sometimes they even used to tease each other about their pretended husbands. When they got older, they started to go to dancing parties. At those days dancing music came from the old-fashioned record player. Mar had lots of boyfriends and Ada, on the other hand, had difficulty making friends. Many times she would just leave Mar at the party and walk back home. One night as she did, she blacked out. She did not know what happened, how long she was gone, or where did she end up. Sub-consciously, she felt that she got lost in the woods, and some other family found her and took her for her own. That seemed to be so long ago, though, as if in another life.

As poor as Ada's family was they had a nanny living with them. She was grandmother Stef's friend. Ada heard the story how ironic Krol's life turned out. She was married but had no children. Then, her husband took ill and passed away. The story went that when Krol was at her husband's funeral, her house burned down, with everything in it. She begged her friend, Stef to take her in her house as the maid because she had no place to go. So, she was taking care of Ada and her siblings, when her parents were working on the farm. Ada's mother used to say that Krol prayed the Holy Rosary around the clock, but heard everything that was going on around her, and sometimes even answered back. Ada did not know the whole story then but, years later, when she heard it from her mother, she understood everything. That woman has lost everything that she had, and the only way she could keep her sanity was to repeat those simple prayers of "Our Father" and "Hail Mary". That was her only consolation, and her only hope in her misery. Krol was babysitting Ada's infant brother, Mare when he got convulsions from a very high fever. Wla blamed her for giving the infant baby the crust from the bread. Ada could not remember if her mother was angry at Krol for that incident but surely she did not mean any harm to the baby. She was a very loving person, with nothing to her name but a small portable chest, like a valise, with a few of her clothing. Her will was that the chest, which was her whole treasure, would go to Mar when she would die.

Mar was Krol's most favored child. Ada always thought that it was because Krol saw the potential future in her. And, indeed, Mar assumed Krol's role in the family, when she was gone. Ada always admired her. She was so good handling her siblings. No mother could have done a better job. She always knew what to do in every situation. When Ada would freeze and was able just to recite the prayer, Mar would always take a positive action. When her brother Acie fell down the steps, no one suspected that he suffered a brain concussion. He fell asleep afterwards and then woke up, throwing up and looking very pale. Mar immediately picked him up from bed, and would not let him fall back asleep. She rushed her father, to get ready, to take him to the hospital. It was wintertime, lots of snow, and four kilometers to walk to the train station, to call the ambulance. Both Mar and her father were taking turns to carry him there. Ada was sure that Mar saved Acie's life. He had a brain concussion but, thanks to Mar's quick thinking, he was alright.

Ada always did all the farm work with her father. If she was not with him, she would always worry about him and wait outside, praying, when it was getting dark. It was all because of that one incident when the horses driven wagon, full of hay, tipped over to a side and fell on her and him. Miraculously, nothing happened to them.

There were two events in the village that overwhelmed Ada with anxieties. They took place almost at the same time. One of them was the contest to honor Lenin who was responsible for the Russian October Revolution of 1917 and creation of Socialism. The contest was based on Lenin's autobiography book. Ada had a photographic memory, and could remember word for word everything that she read. Something happened to her, though, on the day of the contest. She was extremely nervous, her hands were sweaty and, when she picked out the question what sports did Lenin engaged in, she could not think of anything else but nature walks. The judges kept asking her: "and what else, what else"? Ada's answers were: "walking and walking". What was happening to her? She was not on the stage, not at all. She was far away from there. She was following her grandfather, walking slowly through the fields, his hands folded behind his back. Was her grandfather's story of his imprisonment, during the Russian Revolution, coming to life in her mind? And then, there was a moment that Ada was waiting for, and preparing for the longest time, her Confirmation as Jesus' witness and apostle, to spread his Gospel. Ada expected a miracle to happen so she wanted to pray very intensely that the Holy Spirit would enlighten her and do good works through her. At Confirmation, she had the option to confirm the name she has been given at baptism, or choose the name of one of the saints, whose footsteps she would like to follow. Ada chose a controversial name that came as a surprise, even to the pastor that has known her for years. The confirmation took place in another vicinage and all celebrants walked a long way to church there. The whole ritual was a big disappointment to her, though. She could not even remember anything from it, not even who her sponsors were. All she knew that she could not concentrate on her prayers and felt completely empty and cold inside. She left the church tearful. She felt like she missed out on the entire event. From that day on, Ada felt unrest and could hardly hide her constant nervousness.

At social gatherings, it was very common for the family members to tell ghost stories, believed to be true. Ada's sister, Mar had once a very interesting story to share. She was coming home one night and as she approached the very narrow, wooden bridge over the creek she has seen someone standing there. It seemed to be a person, blocking her way and smoking a cigarette. As Mar got close and wondered how she was going to pass by, the apparition or whatever it was, jumped into the water. Mar looked down but could not see anything. Then, the chills went all over her body, and she ran home as fast as she could. Ada did not think that Mar was too scared of ghosts though, for one night she sought refuge at the cemetery, from the drunkards. She was afraid to get beaten up or even raped, when the bunch of drunken men were approaching her. As she quickly looked around, she saw that she was next to the cemetery. Without thinking, she made her way through the cemetery gate and found herself between the tombs. Apparently, that was too much for those intoxicated souls who meant harm to her. They were sure Mar was a ghost and tried to run, stumbling and falling. Mar waited until the coast was clear and then, left the cemetery.

Another interesting story was told by Ada's cousin, Aria's boyfriend. It was nighttime, and he was on his way home. The road went through the woodland, up the hill. Bart spotted a beautiful cat between the trees. He ran up to it calling: "Come on kitty, come on". As he grabbed that "cat", he could not lift it up. Cold sweat was dripping all over him, as he ran inside his aunt's house, nearby. He was pale as a ghost and could not say a word. That was nothing, however, compared to the haunted house of grandmother Stef's brother. The household was terrorized by doors opening at night and someone coming in, by loud banging throughout the night, and dishes falling out from the kitchen cabinets. In the morning, however, everything was intact. Stories from Ada's maternal side of the family were even scarier. Ada's maternal grandfather was a musician. He played violin for a hobby while he worked, full time, as a stone miner. The legend had it that, one night, the entire band of musicians mysteriously disappeared. They were never to be found. Ada's father used to say that animals sensed ghosts much better than humans. He gave creeps everyone at the table, by telling his scary story. He was driving horses at night, when suddenly they stopped and refused to go. They were looking left and right all scared, sniffing and puffing. Ada's father did not see anything, but the horses' behavior made his heart race. It took him a long time to get them going again. Ada, however, never saw anything extraordinary, and was always skeptical of the stories she heard.

"Fear has huge eyes" Ada's mother used to say to her children. She was a very strong woman, able to overcome any obstacles that came her way. As a young girl, she used to work in the preserves factory. One rainy night, as she was walking home from work, with her friend, she was attacked by an "invisible" dog. The animal was invisible to Wla's friend, but to her it was real. Wla was fighting him back with her umbrella, and was screaming for help from her friend. Her friend, however, saw nothing but Wla's umbrella hitting the muddy road. Whatever the phenomenon it was, Wla was able to conquer it and go on. Years and years later, she looked into fear's eyes again. She and her sister Hel were coming home from work at night. As they turned from the main road and crossed the river, they had a feeling that they were being followed. The faster they walked up the hill, the faster the footsteps were behind them. They were near the house already, and Wla decided to take a short cut to her house while Hel continued to go straight. Suddenly Hel gave out a loud shriek, running towards Wla and someone was running right behind her. They both relaxed, as Jon made himself known and apologized for scaring them. Jon was Ada's Aunt Kun's husband. He would always appear in the village, when he was the least expected, sometimes as if from nowhere. Ada always thought then that it had to be some mystery around it. Aunt Kun seemed to be just as mysterious. Numerous times she would send her father a telegram that she was coming. She wanted Ada's father to meet her at the train station and always picked the night hours of arrival. She would never show up, though, and Ada could not look into her father's sad eyes, each time he came back home alone.

Years later, when Ada was on another continent Aunt Kun told Ada about a ghostly apparition of her mother, Stef. Her newborn son Jac was sick and she was exhausted tendering on him and rocking him in the cradle. She closed her eyes to rest up a bit, with the feeling that soon she had to give him his medication. When she opened her eyes again, she realized that she slept through the entire night. It was a beautiful, sunny morning. Puzzled, she looked at the cradle that was still rocking. Suddenly, she realized what was happening and called out: "Mama"? At that she felt a soft breeze in the room, even though the windows were closed. She knew then that indeed it was her mama rocking her baby all night, while she was sleeping.

As much as Ada disbelieved the ghost stories, she could not explain her grandmother Kat's tale of her husband's apparitions. She claimed that her husband came to her one night, apologizing that he left her with ten children. He assured her that he would always be with her, to help her raise them. Every night, she felt him coming to the room. She would move over on the bed, to make room for him.

Grandmother Kat received lump-sum pension money, for her deceased husband. It was a lot of money at those days, and would have made the family rich. Ironically, the day she was paid, the government changed the currency value and what grandmother Kat received was practically nothing. She could do nothing about it but cry. She needed that money so. There was never any food in the house. Sometimes, she would leave the children alone in the house for a week or two, in search of work. If she was lucky, she brought back not only food but some money as well. Other times, there was not enough of food or money in the house, and the children were starving, longing for her return. They would boil some ivy leaves or overgrown mushrooms that were believed to be poisonous. That way they survived until their mother came back. The children went to school only during the spring and autumn, because they had no shoes to cover their feet in the wintertime. Wla was a very good student and made a few attempts to make it to school, in the wintertime. She wrapped her feet in whatever clothing she could find, but it did not work. She could not feel her feet, in the freezing temperatures, and had to run back home.

Grandmother Kat had her mother and brother living in Mecina, not very far from Ada's village. Ada spent a lot of time there, when she was a little girl. Houses were built differently there. Her relative's house was painted all white, on the outside. Ada thought that it looked very nice. She spent many hours in the garden, picking berries. She could eat as many of them as she wanted. It was so peaceful there and green all around. However, when Grandma Kat lost her mother, they stopped coming there so often. Yet, Ada would always remember that white house, surrounded by green trees and bushes.

Ada was always a nature lover, and spent most of her time outdoors. When she had some free time, she enjoyed picking fresh apples from the trees in the orchard, or currant berries. Black currants were thought to be good for the heart. Ada's mother used to sell apples and currants at the marketplace in the city. Many other goods she would sell there as well. In the season, Ada and her mother would go miles from home, in the forest, to pick blackberries, blueberries, raspberries, and wild strawberries. They would come back, carrying in both hands large buckets of berries, ready to be sold at the market. During the summer, Ada's mother also used to sell mushrooms that Ada picked in the forest. Ada would get up very early in the morning to go mushroom picking. There were only certain areas in the forest that would grow them and Ada knew exactly where to look. Golden chanterelles, porcini or cep, were only some of the edible mushrooms that Ada would pick. There were few others that Ada knew they were good to eat, but did not know what they were called. The most impressive, healthy mushrooms were sold fresh, others were dried in the sun and sold later, and some were used in the household, to make delicious mushroom soups and gravies. Mushrooms could sometimes be found in the most unpredictable places. Ada was pleasantly surprised, when she found enormous, healthy mushrooms on the lawn by the oak tree, near the creek by her house. There were so many of them. They had brown heads, with the brownish-white stems. Ada's family used to call them "prawdziwki", meaning "real mushrooms". It was only that one summer season that those mushrooms popped up, under the oak tree. Ada would check the area frequently each summer, but could find none anymore.

Sometimes Ada's family had visitors for the summer. They were Ada's cousins. It was difficult to do any farm work, having the city cousins around. They knew nothing about it, even though they were willing to help. Zdi and Zby were trying to find any entertainment they could. They liked to swim, but there were no lakes around. To Ada's surprise, however, they built a dam on the creek, and had a sort of a swimming pool. Ada never tried to swim but, one day, could not resist her cousins' temptations and went in the water. She almost drowned, even though the water was not high at all. Both of her cousins had a laugh of their lifetime. Ada was always very sensitive of people laughing at her, so on her way back from the creek she took out her anger on her neighbor's tree. What was she thinking? Apparently, she did not give it any thought, and started ripping off the young branches of the tree. The neighbor ran out and started screaming at her. Ada ran away and, from that day on, she was never able to look into her neighbor's eyes again. She was so embarrassed that she wished to be invisible, every time she saw him.

Since Ada seemed to be always a loner, her mother thought that the dancing lessons would bring her out of her shell and signed her up for classes. As much as Ada would love to belong to a dance club, though, she could not follow the steps. She did everything opposite to what the teacher and her dance partners did. She was so embarrassed that she refused to ever go again. He sister, Mar took her place. Ada's mom did not give up on her, though. She signed her up for another course: knitting, crocheting, embroidery, and sewing. Ada was very poor at that too. She managed to do only a few things, despite her sweaty hands that kept the thread wet and tangled up. She did well, though, in taking notes. Ada helped her mother with taking notes while Wla was showing her how to follow directions to make things.

It was incredible that this timid, afraid of everything, simple, rural girl would find her way to America. However, what seemed to be a dream come true turned out to be a life in hell for Ada. Even her father thought that his daughter would have a bright future at his cousin's house, so he dared to share with her a prospect that she may find her true love on another continent, as his many cousins in America had children of their own, her age. He had no idea that his cousin's husband had hidden, bad intentions from the time they invited her over. It all seemed wonderful to Ada at first. They appeared to be childless, affectionate couple and Uncle Woo asked her that she would refer to him and his wife as mom and dad. That did not seem to bother Ada, though, because in English language it was kind of meaningless to her. But when he started making the advances at her, the paradox was killing her. How could one expect to be a father figure and at the same time a lover? Uncle Woo would weigh Ada every other day, too. It was so humiliating to her. She felt like she was a guinea pig, each time she had to step up on that scale. What was the purpose of it? What were her relatives trying to tell her by that? Yes, in the first few days, Ada gained some weight but soon the emotional stress got the best of her and she was getting very thin. She met Auntie Sun's friend, Ethie once. Ethie, who once admired Ada in her homeland, wanted to help her out and get her a job in a packaging company. It was not up to Ada, however. Ada sensed that Ethie knew that something was wrong there and she never saw her again.

Auntie Sun found Ada three cleaning jobs which cheered her up a bit because at least she could help her family abroad by sending them all of her earnings. One of her jobs was near Auntie Sun's house. Most of the times Ada got a ride, however. She waited near the private school, where Lola dropped off her two children every morning. Ada was not sure, but Lola appeared to be a single mother. Her house was very poor, compared to the other two mansions that Ada cleaned. Yet, Lola paid her twenty dollars a day while the others paid her only fifteen. No one has watched her at Lola's house. She was free to leave whenever she was done. However, it took her a whole day to do the cleaning, because the vacuum cleaner did not work properly, and she was cleaning the carpeting with a wet rag. Lola and her children were very sweet. They treated her like one of the family, not as a housekeeper. Each time Ada was making Tim's and Ann's beds, she was thinking of her homeland, and of her younger brothers and sisters. Needless to say, she missed them more than ever.

Lola used to tell Ada not to be shy and make herself a sandwich for lunch. There was hardly anything in the refrigerator, though. Ada picked up a jar, with "peanut butter" written on it. She tasted it but could not swallow it and was choking on it. "How could anyone eat that?" She wondered. When Lola's schedule changed, she gave Ada keys to her house. Something was wrong with the lock, though, and every morning Ada had trouble opening the door. Then, one day, as she tried to open it, the lock fell out. Ada thought that it was her fault, that she broke it. At first, she wanted to turn back and leave, but then decided to clean the house, anyway. The whole time she was thinking of the broken lock and felt terrible. When she was finally done, she wrote a brief note to Lola, and left the twenty dollars inside of it. She told Lola that she could not take the money because she broke the lock. Ada forgot all about the children, though. When they got home from school and saw the door opened, they got very scared, thinking that someone broke into their house. Lola rushed home from work, alarmed by them. She found Ada's note on the counter. Ada's heart almost stopped, when Lola called. However, she was not angry with her. In fact, she knew that the lock was no good and needed to be replaced but she neglected it for the longest time. She wished, though, that Ada would have left a note on the door for Tim and Ann, to spare them the fright.

And then, there were Pam's & Jean's mansions. Ada has never seen anything like that before. It could not even compare to the kings' castle that she once saw on the school trip in her own country. How could some people live so extravagant? Ada thought. Everything was so rich and elegant. Ada was so impressed when she saw Pam press a button on the remote control, to open the garage door. Everything in the house seemed to be remote controlled too, even the laundry shuffle on each floor and the garbage disposal in the kitchen. The carpeting was so fine and thick. Everything in each room matched: from the carpeting, to the furniture, paintings on the walls, and draperies. Even the bedding in the bedrooms matched the rest of the furnishings. Ada was afraid to touch anything in the house. She took her time dusting and vacuuming. It seemed that there was not even any dust on the furniture and the carpet looked clean, but she did it anyway. After all, that's what she was being paid for. The kitchen was usually clean too. Occasionally, there were just a few dishes, but all she had to do was to rinse them and put them in the dishwasher. The kitchen was truly gorgeous. There were so many cabinets and the kitchen counter was very long. They had to be custom made, just like the rest of the furnishings in the house. The kitchen tile matched the walls and the cabinets. Jean's mansion was just as elegant as Pam's. That was truly how America was portrayed in Ada's homeland.

Auntie Sun also sponsored Ada so she could permanently stay in America. However, she needed a proof that she did the housework in her homeland. She asked her Aunt Kun, who was a notary public, to send her the paper.

After all, Ada spent one summer over her house, helping her out. Needless to say, Ada mentioned in the letter to her mother that she asked Aunt Kun for the certificate she needed. Then, her mother sent her a certificate as well. Auntie Sun gave those papers relating to Ada's immigration to the agency that was handling her case.

When Ada received a notice to appear in the immigration office for an interview, she panicked because she was not sure which certificate the agency submitted. Her feelings were right because the interview turned out to be a total disaster. Since Ada did not know which certificate the agency submitted, she relied on her intuition which let her down. When she realized that she was talking of the wrong employer, she tried to patch things up, explaining that she worked for Aunt Kun during her summer vacation and did housework for Mrs. Maria, in her village, during the school year. The interviewer wanted to know the exact days and hours, after or before classes that she worked for Mrs. Maria. At the end, Ada had to provide another certificate from Mrs. Maria, with the exact days and hours that she worked for her.

Auntie Sun's sister and her entire family would frequently visit over the weekend. They had a station wagon that fit all eight of them. During those visits, Ada missed her family back home more than ever. For two days the cousins took over the entire house. They felt very much at home. Her teenage cousins did pretty much whatever they wanted. The house looked so messy, but they cleaned everything up before they left.   Uncle Jon was a tractor trailer driver and made good money, so his wife did not have to work. He was not fond of Ada and sometimes said cruel things to her. Auntie Sun often bragged how good Ada was doing at school.   Uncle Jon would then test her how smart she was. He was telling her that she would be having difficulty expressing herself because in English language almost every word had many meanings to it. He was also wearing a brace on one of his legs but Ada never questioned why.

This new world that Ada faced was totally different from what she was used to. Having relatives at Auntie Sun's and Uncle Woo's house did not bother Ada as much as taking trips with them.   She had to go with them everywhere they went. Usually they would go to Avoca, where most of Auntie Sun's siblings lived. At the beginning, Ada liked it. The scenery reminded her of her village. Her cousins even took her to the movies once. Ada did not know that it was an "X" rated movie, with a lot of violence in it. She could not watch movies like that and came back home very sick, with a terrible headache and nausea. There was, yet, another reason why she did not mind going to Avoca, in the first few months in America.   She liked one of her cousins, Mare. He was the son of Auntie Sun's brother. Ada liked to play volley ball with her cousins, as long as Mare was participating.   She remembered her father's words: "My cousins in America have children too and perhaps you may fall in love with one of them." Ada tried to talk to Mare, whenever she had a chance, but soon realized that he had no interest in her. She was heartbroken.

Another man broke Ada's heart, too. It was Uncle Woo's nephew. He was only a few years older than Ada. He took Ada to the City of New York, with his friend Scar. Ada waited for that moment for months and already gave up hope that she would ever see that legendary city. She was very excited then, when Ben offered to take her. They had a very good time together and Ada hoped he would ask her out. Ben did ask her out one more time but for a car show in the City. Ada was not interested in cars and was walking around very tired and disappointed. Anyway, she was not alone with Ben. His friend, Scar was with him again. It had to be about midnight, when they were leaving the show. Something has happened. Ada lost the sight of them for a moment and was about to panic, when they appeared. They did not seem the same, though. They were laughing and giving Ada strange looks. Where they laughing at her? What just have happened? Ada wondered.

While at High School, Ada worked very hard to keep up her grades. She was grateful to the school principal, for allowing her to finish the twelfth grade. According to High School regulations, the student had to have attended the given school for two years, in order to graduate from that school. Ada did not stand a chance to attend the day school for two years, because that would make her twenty one on the graduation, and the maximum graduation age for the day school was twenty.

After merely a week at school, Ada was called to the principal's office. When she realized that she might not be permitted to finish her twelfth grade, she quickly spoke on her own behalf. She pulled out all of the quizzes she had. She aced them all. When the principal saw how well she was doing and how much it meant for her to graduate, she said she would make an exception for her. Ada could not thank her enough. She still had the language barrier but did not mind to study long hours. She knew that Auntie Sun and Uncle Woo would not send her to college so she had to prepare herself, the best she could, to get a job after High School. She was lucky she took typewriting because all of her senior term papers had to be typed. Stenography helped her to master the language but she would not have the use of it in the office. At the finals, when the teacher was speaking fast, Ada could hardly catch the words said and had trouble writing the entire sentences in shorthand. She did the best in accounting. Even though she never used the adding machine, she always got her answers right.

Ada liked her English class, too and did very good in it, despite the fact that she was a newcomer. There were many term papers that she did in English, including one on the poetry. The poetry theme that Ada picked was spring. She analyzed beautiful poems that were written by the famous authors. Her analysis truly presented the beauty and joy of that wonderful season of the year. Another term paper was to analyze the book "The Old Man and the Sea". Ada summarized, not only the main theme and the moral of the book, but also emphasized the irony of life that the main character of the book represented. Just as she did in the poetry assignment, Ada also analyzed the style of writing: similes, repetitions, and other various writing techniques. Some assignments had to be presented orally. Ada was very nervous when she had to speak but she did very well on the fictitious advertisement she had to present. She based her advertisement on the phrase that her mother used to say, when the children were asking for something that was impossible for them to get. She would say: "And what else would you wish for, heavenly almonds?" Ada's vocabulary was still poor and she could not find the translation for "heavenly". So her advertisement did not, in fact, reflect her mother's saying and ended: "Just remember: Hawaiian, blue, almonds, and me." As for the health class, Ada had rather low grades. She could not comprehend it. Also, she was troubled by the book that the health teacher passed around, "All about Sex." She did not read the book, but just glanced on some of the pages. She felt ashamed and wondered: "How could the teacher hand the students a book like that?" Ironically, shortly after, that same teacher passed away.

Ada was friendly with everyone at school, and no one bothered her. In the Study Hall she did all, or most, of her homework. In cafeteria, she usually sat next to a girl in the wheelchair. They often conversed about school and their families. Sometimes Ada was doing her homework and kept quiet. Teachers admired her but speculated, too, that there was something troublesome about her home. Auntie Sun had to take Ada to the doctor one time, when she developed a large sore on her thigh. The gym teacher thought it could be contagious, and told Ada that she could not come back to school without a doctor's note. The doctor told Auntie Sun that there was nothing wrong with her, though. "The sore that she developed", the doctor said, "was from her nervousness". Ada's classmates never questioned her about the sore. It seemed that they all liked her. Most of them signed her yearbook, too, and hoped to keep in touch. Ada was also awarded two scholarships, compliments of her two teachers. One of them was the Perseverance Award and the other, Business Education Award. Those were monetary awards, two twenty dollar bills.

When Ada graduated from High School, she found a job in the office. There she fell in love with Phil, from the first day she saw him. However, she was not sure if he had the same feelings towards her. Every time he walked into the office, her heart was pounding. She was very nervous and she would drop things. Sadly, she learned he loved her too, when he was leaving for another job. Ada would never forget that day. He asked her if she would have lunch with him. They went to the second floor offices. He took Ada's hand and told her that he was in love with her. Ada trembled, when his lips touched hers. Her heart was beating so fast that she could hardly breathe. They talked and laughed, holding each other's hands. That was a long lunch. Ada wondered if her boss, Dor and her sister suspected anything. Finally, Ada had to say goodbye. Phil took Ada's home telephone number, but did he ever call? Ada would never know. She was not allowed to pick up the phone and suddenly there were so many "wrong number" calls. Ada could not stop thinking about Phil. It seemed that nothing could cheer her up. The thought that it could have been Phil calling and was told that he had a wrong number was killing her. How did that make him feel? Perhaps, he was just as miserable as she was. However, there was nothing she could do about it. He never gave her his home address or telephone number.

Ada overcame her heartache when Uncle Woo's nephew from Poland came to visit. When she first learned that he was coming for a summer vacation, she was very angry. He did not even arrive yet and Auntie Sun and Uncle Woo were already making plans of marrying her to him. She swore to herself then that she would not even look at him. However, when he arrived she could not help but to fall in love with him because he was so handsome and gentle. Her happiness did not last for long, though, because this loving, gentle man turned against her and repeated everything that she confided in him to his aunt and uncle. Uncle Woo threatened to kill her so she ran away from them. She spent one night at her friend, Ali's house and the next day, with her help, found one room apartment to stay.

It was there that she was visited by the pastor from her village, Msgr. Stan. He claimed that he came to America to visit his relatives and just stopped to see her but Ada was convinced that she was the purpose of his whole trip. He wanted to help her and her family with the crisis that he learned about from her parents. Wla and Gien were devastated because they received a telegram from Auntie Sun that Ada has gone mad and was on drugs or something and they did not know of her whereabouts.

Ada noticed that the pastor was a very down to earth person. She was surprised, too, when she saw him wearing jeans. That was on the trip that they all took to Blessed Mary's holy sanctuary that was a replica of that in Ada's homeland. Ali's husband drove them there. Ada cooked meals for Father Stan and they both had so much to talk about. Father Stan was very happy to see that there was nothing wrong with her. As for the sleeping arrangements, she made them beforehand, in the rectory of the church that she belonged to.   Each day that he stayed there, he celebrated the morning mass and was chanting all the readings, instead of speaking. Ada liked it so much. It felt like she was in her home village again.

Even though Ada was at war with Auntie Sun and Uncle Woo, she let them know about Father Stan's visit. They insisted on meeting him. Ada was invited to come, too. At dinner table, Auntie Sun and Uncle Woo could not stop talking about their two dogs; how smart they were, what they ate, where they slept, and how affectionate they were. It was obvious that they treated their dogs like children. Father Stan felt uncomfortable. He was not accustomed to pets being treated like humans. Auntie Sun and Uncle Woo also invited him on the trip to New York. Ada also went and really enjoyed it, especially the cruise on a boat around Manhattan Skyline. Throughout the whole time with Father Stan, Auntie Sun and Uncle Woo not even once mentioned the telegram to Ada's parents or Ada's subject overall.

When Father Stan left, Ada really had no one to talk to. Her friend, Ali had problems of her own. She stayed home with her four children. She cooked and did her house chores while her husband was at work. Ada noticed that she was addicted to television shows, too, but that was her only entertainment she had. The couple also often quarreled about money. Ali had to account for every penny that Stan gave her. If she bought something for herself, she was in trouble. She liked to dress nicely and buy something new every once in a while but Ada knew she shopped wisely and always looked for bargains.

In need to talk to someone, Ada contacted one of her teachers from High School. She thought that he might be of some help to her. After all, he was the one that referred her to the accounting firm that she was working for. He was of Polish descent and Ada used to be in his typing class. Ada called him in a wrong time, though. His son was being ordained for a priest that day. However, he scheduled to meet with her, in couple of days after that. She told him that she moved out from Auntie Sun's house but did not get into much detail. The teacher told her that he would like her to write down her goals in life. When they met the second time, Ada gave him a piece of paper with her goals. She was very lonely so, as her first goal, she put down that she would like to have the family of her own. Since she always so admired the City of New York, she could also see herself living there, in one of the tallest buildings. She put down as well that she would like to become a bookkeeper because that kind of work always fascinated her and she was doing so well in it at High School. Ada could not remember what else she wrote on that piece of paper that she gave to her typing teacher but she never saw him again.

Since Ada could not think of anyone else, she went to see her grandmother Stef's sister, Aunt Roz. Roz claimed that she could read the future from one's hand. When she took Ada's hand, though, she suddenly changed. She looked pale and somewhat troubled. Ada insisted that she would tell her what she saw. Aunt Roz, then, told her that she could not find on her hand the line of life. She suggested that Ada would spend the night with her. However, even though Aunt Roz was very sympathetic to Ada, there was nothing she could do for her. She could hardly help herself for she was old and had a pacemaker, after she suffered from a heart attack. The best advice she could give Ada was to make peace with Auntie Sun and Uncle Woo.

So, Ada fulfilled her destiny by moving back with Auntie Sun and Uncle Woo and marrying Fes the next year, when he came back. The day of her wedding Fes got so drunk that he did not know what he was doing. Ada felt so alone and so scared. Her wedding night she spent watching over her husband, petrified that he may die from alcohol overdose. The next day Fes felt better. They opened their wedding cards. Ada realized that the money gifts they received would not even pay for her wedding gown and the pictures. She cleaned Fes' rented tuxedo, the best she could, and headed to Auntie Sun to return it. On the way she passed a Memorial Day parade. It was a festive view, too much for Ada who was hurting inside and wondering what the future would bring. Her wedding day would indeed be never forgotten.

Ada found some sympathy in Auntie Sun. She told Ada that all guests at the wedding reception, seeing what was happening, were opening their wedding cards and putting a lesser amount of money in them, usually fifteen dollars. Ada then understood why her wedding gifts were less than generous. Auntie Sun finally realized, too, that Fes was playing two cards. He would be telling Ada one thing and another to Auntie Sun and Uncle Woo, anything to cause friction. He even told Ada to take from Auntie Sun's house an old record player and then told them that she took it. As a result, Auntie Sun demanded that Ada would return her house keys. Ada gave them to her; she had no intention of keeping them in the first place. She returned the old record player as well.

Fes kept on hanging out with his cousin, Ben. He tried to keep Ada away from him, though, and would get infuriated if Ada spoke English, in Ben's presence. So Ada spoke only in her native language, to keep peace. In the meantime, Fes was taking English classes. There he met Ceyu and the two became drinking buddies. Ada had hard feelings towards Ben's mother for allowing Fes to hang out there with him and drink but deeply inside knew that no one forced Fes to do it. Then, one night, Fes called Ada to pick him up at Aunt Hel's house. When she got there, he and Ceyu were already gone. Ada was driving back and forth like a maniac, trying to find them. Finally, she caught up with them, near her house. They were both very drunk and Ada was amazed that they made their way home. After all, it was quite a few miles to walk. There was trouble, however. They were both arguing on account of Ada. On the way, Ceyu was betting that she would not pick up Fes and that she did not care for him. When Ada brought them home, Fes wanted to arm wrestle with Ceyu. However, Ceyu managed to get his arm down and Fes started punching him. Ada screamed and held Fes back, asking Ceyu to hurry up and leave.

Fes continued drinking with his cousin and Ada was so pitiful, trying to get him out of bars once she'd find him. One time, she found him totally intoxicated and openly flirting with a girl. He seemed not to have noticed Ada and gave her no mind. Onie told her that Fes has been fondling her all night. She knew that she was hurting Ada but did not care. She told Ada: "Can't you see that he loves me and not you?" Ada was all shaken up and left the bar. Fes' cousin came running after her, trying to calm her down. Ben's words were no consolation to her, though. Actually, it felt, as if they were piercing her heart. She would so much want to blame Ben for her troubles but deeply inside she knew the truth. Ada was convinced that under alcohol influence one is really capable to lose all of his senses and, thus, not responsible for his actions. So, she would not give up on Fes and continued to worry about him. She went as far as calling the police one night and asking if, by any chance, there were any accidents reported because he did not show up home.

And, then, there was Zela. Fes seemed to like her company and spent a lot of time with her. Sometimes he would bring home all three of them: Zela, her brother, and her mother. Deeply inside, Ada knew that the trio was just a cover up. They lived in an apartment building, near the city park. Fes would always invite Ada to go visit them but she could tell it was only for Fes to look good in Zela's mother's eyes. Ada was broken hearted once, seeing Zela playing Frisbee with Fes. Being pregnant did not make Ada handicapped, did it? She so much wanted to be a part of that game! Zela also liked to drink with Fes. Why did Ada put up with all that? After all, that was her home too. The truth was that she was afraid of Fes and had nowhere to turn. There was a time when Zela, as drunk as Fes, went to bed with him and Ada had no choice but to lie down between them two. She wanted to be sure that nothing happened. What good did that do, though? Fes always bragged how many girls he had before he married Ada. She would never answer. Fes was the first man that Ada had intercourse with and would never forget how painful it was. Her husband was too drunk, though, to even notice that.

Fes would never change and would cause friction everywhere they went. Ty was no different. He stirred things up between her and her grandmother so much that when Ada and Fes moved out, she moved out too. Ty wanted to live with Ada and Fes but Ada would not allow that. She knew that two women in the same house would be nothing but trouble. Even though she was heartbroken about the whole Ty situation, she helped her to get a place to stay and to open a bank account. Mrs. Nerakiy gave her granddaughter all the money she saved for her over the years. Ada and Fes did not leave Mrs. Nerakiy's house on good terms. It was such a shame. She and her family were so nice to Ada! They surprised Ada and Fes with the wedding anniversary wishes and a song on the radio once. They also came to Acil's 1st Birthday party. There was nothing, though, that Ada could do so she would just pray that the things would work out for Ty and Mrs. Nerakiy's "wound" would soon be healed.

After seven years of being away from her family in Poland, Ada surprised them and came back for a two week visit, with her husband and one year old daughter. It was on November 1, 1981, during the state of emergency in her country. That was the last time that she saw her father because just a few months after that visit he became seriously ill and died. She could never forgive herself for not being there by her father's side. She wept for days but what good did that do? She knew she could not bring him back. So, when her son was born, she named him after her father. She could not have been happier. When she was holding her newborn baby, close to her, she felt so much joy and was so much at peace. She thought her baby was beautiful and looked so much like her father. Anon was such a quiet baby. He hardly ever cried and was content with every little attention that he got. Ada would never forget the day she gave birth to him. It was very early in the morning, around three o'clock. Later in the day, Fes came to visit with Acil. When Acil looked at Ada holding the newborn baby, she started to cry. Was she jealous of Anon or did she miss Ada so much? Ada gave the baby to Fes to hold and picked up Acil. She was talking to her in the sweet voice: "Look Acil, you have a brother. Before you know, you will be playing with him and will never be lonely. And I want you to know that I love you with my whole heart. Don't be afraid that the baby will take me away from you." She kept hugging and kissing Acil. Finally, Acil wanted to be put down. She wanted to hold the baby. Ada let her do that but was right next to her, making sure that the baby was secure in her arms.

Ada wanted to spend time with her newborn baby. She was tired of paperwork. Anon was always so happy in her arms. As little as he was, he kept smiling at her. His smile brought so much warmth to Ada's home. It's been a while since Acil was an infant but Ada did not lose her touch yet. It all came back to her naturally. Even though, by nature, Ada was rather clumsy, she did alright feeding, holding, and changing the baby. She was extra careful when she held him, making sure that his head was always supported by her arm. Throughout her pregnancy, Ada had a feeling that she was carrying a son. Now that he was born, she was ecstatic. She had a pair, a girl and a boy.

By coincidence or not, Ada was having dreams of her father. It was the same each time she had it. She would come to visit her family in Poland and her father would come out to greet her. She would throw her arms around him, happy to see him alive, for, subconsciously, in her dream she knew that he passed away. She wrote to her mother about it. Soon, Ada would learn that her mom had a dream about her father, too. In her dream he came to her and brought a beautiful bouquet of flowers. He told her that he was very happy. Ada did not know where the dreams came from but was happy to dream of something so wonderful, rather than having a nightmare.

Anon was a beautiful baby and everyone admired him. Ada wanted Auntie Sun and Uncle Woo to attend his baptism. However, that did not happen, for Fes messed up things again. They went to Zela's house and it just so happened that they had a visitor. That woman knew Auntie Sun and Uncle Woo and Fes made a remark to her: "With family, one looks the best only on the pictures." Ada found out at work, from the company owner's wife that Fes' statement went back to Auntie Sun and Uncle Woo and they were very hurt by it. Needless to say, they ignored the invitation to come to Anon's baptism. Ada felt guilty, even though the statement did not come from her. She also felt somewhat responsible for Auntie Sun's heart attack. She learned about it from the priest that came to bless their home. It was the custom that came from Ada's native country of Poland. Acil was just about crawling then. Ada was relieved, then, when the priest concluded that Auntie Sun survived the attack and was doing alright. Now, too, she felt bad about Fes' remark. None of Fes' family came to the baptism. Only a handful of Ada's and Fes' friends joined the celebration.

Soon after that, Ada suffered from the nervous breakdown. She could not stop her mind from wandering, could not sleep and lost her appetite. Since there was no one to help, she was quickly deteriorating and became delusional. Needless to say, she ended up in the hospital. She did not completely lose touch with reality, though, and was aware of everything that was going on around her. She felt trapped in that mental hospital and felt heartbroken. On her first day in the hospital, when she was holding for Fes to come to the phone, she heard Christmas songs. "Christmas in March?" She wondered. When her husband came to visit her, he was telling her that something strange was going on at his place of work. The elevator got stuck, and he was asked to open it. He tried the key, but it did not work. Later on, when Ada came home, she thought, she has been seeing posters saying: "You lost your keys in A18." She wondered: "What was the meaning of it? Did my husband have an affair with that woman at A18?" She also thought she has been seeing stacks of correspondence, with Anon's name on it. "It couldn't be real, could it?" Ada knew, though, she was really in a bad shape and was imagining things. She even thought that she saw the writing in blood on her apartment door. It seemed to her that she went back in centuries, to the time when the Angel of God took away lives of all the first-borns, but passed over the doors marked with blood. She was paranoid. Was it for real? Was there really any writing, or was it just her mind playing tricks on her? She, then, looked at the shoe box and could have sworn that the signature on it was that of her father's. She could easily distinguish "Jan" in it. She was getting more and more delusional. All the inanimate things around her seemed to be moving and her daughter's clown seemed to be laughing at her. Ada was terrified. She thought that the world was coming to the end and the judgment day was near. Acil was furiously banging on the drums that Fes bought her and Ada felt it was the Angel of Death gathering and separating the sheep from the goats like the Bible prophesized. As if in response to her track of thinking, she heard a chorus singing. She could not tell whether it was coming from outside or the apartment below her but she could tell that they were church hymns to Virgin Mary. Overpowered with fear, she started to recite the Lord's Prayer. For some unknown reason, she recollected her catechism class in High School. It was a discussion of different religious groups in the world. The priest seemed to be implying that each religion taught the basic principles of life, the right and wrong. Although she was catholic and the Bible was clear that only those who believed that by participating in the Holy Communion, only those eating the symbolic bread of body of Jesus and drinking the symbolic wine of blood of Jesus Christ could be saved, she was somehow doubtful. "How can a righteous person be damned, just because he is not catholic?" She began to pray aloud, reflecting on each word: "Our Father, who art in heaven, hallowed be Thy name; Thy kingdom come; Thy will be done on earth as it is in heaven. Give us this day our daily bread and forgive us our trespasses as we forgive those who trespass against us. And lead us not into temptation but deliver us from evil." At that Ada saw a cover of a music disc, with Pope John II picture on it. She was tempted to play it. She thought that she was going to hear Pope's preaching and the church songs. As she turned the music on, she almost passed out. It was some devilish music. She looked on the record cover again and saw the name "God's Spell" written across. She trembled with fear, remembering the night of the Spell in her village in Kamionka years ago. She put herself together, though. "I have nothing to fear. I don't feel that I did anything wrong." She once more thought of the "Lord's Prayer" and the spell was broken. She went to pick up Anon from the crib. For the first time, in the long time, she was able to smile.

Two years later, in 1986, Ada suffered from another nervous breakdown. She was hospitalized, again, when she was living through her imaginary 3rd World War. When she woke up in the morning, after spending the night in the emergency room, she heard someone crying for help. She did not even notice before that there was another person in the room. That young, dark skin girl was strapped to bed. With her weak voice, she asked for some water. Ada took a cup that was next to her bed, and went to the bathroom to fill it up with water. She was holding it, while her roommate was drinking. Then, two policemen came to take her away. Ada could not picture that young girl doing anything wrong, and said aloud: "She didn't do anything." The cops answered with anger: "Let her explain it to the judge!" Ada was subjected to many trials, in the hospital itself when she found herself caught up in the "Annie" play and, then, when she was transferred to Carrier for her long term treatment. She survived, though, as she always did because of her faith and the love for her children.

Then, it was 1989, the year of Ada's third child, Esse's birth. It was only eleven days before Christmas and, indeed, a Holiday for Ada. She was so much at peace. When she held her in her arms, she felt like she was in Paradise. Everything looked so wonderful to her and she even thought she saw magazines laying around, with Christmas written on the cover page and her baby's picture on it. Indeed, in the hospital everyone called Esse the princess. Ada thought that it was because the nurses were angry, for Dr. Poch told them they were to use only cotton sheets for her, since she developed a sore on her nose. It was from her poking the nose against the sheet. What was she trying to do, lift her head up already? She looked so cute doing that. Ada had Esse in her room almost all the time. When she held her, she felt so peaceful, as if two hearts were united in one. However, she was waiting for Fes to come. Where was he? What was taking him so long to come, to see his new addition to the family? Was he not as excited with Esse as she was? Finally, Fes showed up. He told Ada that he has been painting the rooms. "It was supposed to be a surprise", he said. Ada's eyes got misty. "The rooms were fine", she thought. She just painted them with her mother two months ago. Was it not far more important for Fes to be by her side?

A few months before Esse was born, Ada's mom visited them. She brought so much joy to Ada's life. For once, in all those miserable years, Ada had someone close to talk to. Acil and Anon loved their grandmother, too. Acil was especially close to her. She knew some of the Polish language that she learned from her babysitter, enough words to communicate. Wla and Acil would explore the entire City of Eli. They visited all the stores. Ada's mom bought a lot of things to bring back home. Among others, she bought two beautiful religious paintings. Years later, when Ada was visiting her family, she saw one of the paintings framed and hanging on the wall. Wla had a large, almost a perfect square room. The painting was so big that took most of the space on the wall. It looked really beautiful. The other painting Ada's mom gave to Akin.

During her mother's stay, Ada had it really good. While she was at work, her mother cleaned, washed clothes and cooked dinner. Yet, the most important were the moments that Ada and her mom spent together. Ada had her mother all to herself. She could get as much emotional and close to her as she wanted. They had night-long conversations, about so many good things. Bad times they did not want to remember or talk about. Fes worked an evening shift at that time. One morning when Ada got up, she saw that the door to her apartment was opened. It was just the chain on the door that kept it from opening all the way. Ada got scared, when she could not find Fes. It became obvious to her that he could not get home when he came from work around midnight because someone put the chain on the door. Ada's mom admitted to putting it on. She just wasn't thinking. Ada became hysterical. She ran outside. The first thing that came to her mind was to check the car. She found it and, with her heart pounding, she peaked inside. To her relief, Fes was inside, sleeping on the back seat. She knocked on the window and woke him up. She apologized to him for locking him out. When they came home, Ada's mom was crying. Ada put her arms around her and kissed her. She was so sorry that she overreacted and perhaps made her mother feel very bad. It was so like Ada, though, always so worried about everything, especially her family.

Fes and Ada's mom were very much getting along. Ada was happy to see that because it made her mom's stay so much more pleasurable. Wla still held a grudge against Auntie Sun and Uncle Woo, for the telegram they sent, when Ada ran away from them, and for the picture exposing Ada's breasts. Ada's mom knew that the picture was taken when Ada was so much in distress. What gave them the right to spread ugly rumors around the family and throughout the City of Eli where Ada lived? However, those hard feelings did not stop Wla from visiting Auntie Sun and Uncle Woo. They did not make a good impression on her, though. Wla also met their niece who stayed with them, while she attended college. She did not know that this grown woman now once as a little girl was the only one that had pity on Ada who was near breakdown, before her own wedding. It was Ron who, without a word, handed her a cup of water and her facial expression was saying: "Please stop crying". Ada's mom was also pleased to meet Fes's sister, Hel and her two children. She knew them from before, though, for they spent a few days vacationing at her house once, before they came to America.

In 1992 Ada took a trip to her home country with Anon and Esse. It was hard on the children because they did not know any Polish. They were so happy, then, when they came to Fes' sister, Enia's house. Anon was pleased because her daughters spoke perfect English. Finally, he had someone to communicate with. His cousins were eager to know what his life was like in the United States and inquired about Acil who stayed back with her father. They were also flying paper-made airplanes and played different games with Anon. Enia made dinner for Ada's family. They were all watching Esse eating her chicken soup, with such an appetite as if she did not eat for days. Enia spent a lot of time talking to Ada's mom. She did not quite get over her mother's death. As Jan was dying from cancer, it seemed that there was no room for her in her son's house where she lived before or her two daughters' that lived nearby. Enia took her in and nursed her, as best as she could. It was too much on her, as well as on the rest of her family, to watch her mother's months-long suffering. Ada's sister, Tila was like a God-sent Angel. She came every day by train that took a few hours, to take care of Jan. Each time she came she would wash her, change the bedding, and clean her wound. She would also give her an injection of morphine to stop her pain. Then, as Jan's condition worsened, Tila arranged for a priest to come, to give her the last sacrament. She thought that Jan would object to it but to her surprise, Jan was relieved. In fact, she was happy that she was able to make the last reconciliation, before her death. Tila was the only one that witnessed it but would never reveal it to anyone.

Ada also heard Enia telling her mom one of the principles that she taught her daughters: "Don't ever tell a lie. If you don't want to tell the truth and don't want to lie, just don't say anything, simply keep quiet".

All the wrongdoings that Ada experienced from other people did not stop her from helping those in trouble. On her job in 1995 Bea was not doing any work at all. Besides gossiping with Onie, she was coming to work late or leaving early. One morning, she called that she would be late because she had a dentist appointment. She did not show up until late in the afternoon. Ada was very worried about her. Wondering what could have happened to her, she was praying silently for her. Finally, Bea came in. She claimed that she fell asleep in the dentist's office. She seemed to be somehow different and was playing with Ada's mind by saying: "I found my way to the office with no problem, and being outside did not bother me. It is completely absurd to believe that there is a twilight zone out there." Ada sensed that the owner was very unhappy with Bea and when she did not call and did not arrive at work the next day, he wanted to fire her. Ada heard him telling Onie to write her termination letter. She felt very bad for Bea who was almost of retirement age. Then, she got a brainstorm. Didn't Bea fall under her desk a day before? She got up quickly and did not tell anyone about it because she was probably embarrassed. "That's it", Ada thought. "This should save Bea." Ada approached the owner and told him about Bea's accident the day before. "She must be hurt and that's why she did not call or come to work", said Ada. Immediately, the owner got on the phone with Bea. Now, he was concerned about her well being and she was being treated like a queen when she came back to work.

While working at NEAT, Ada had a privilege to attend her boss' wedding. She bought a black gown, sparkling with gold. She was very thin then and the gown fitted her perfectly. She always had good taste in clothing. Everyone thought she looked stunning, in her sparkling gown, with matching gold shoes, earrings, and a necklace. Ada never wore jewelry, so no one was used to her new appearance. She also got a haircut and the beautician did a marvelous job. Ada's short hair, with the front left side layered, perfectly matched her complexion. Onie seemed envious of Ada, as she said: "Oh, I don't want to look better than the bride." She and Ada shared the same room in the hotel. The wedding was very festive. After all, the company owner was a multi millionaire. He even owned his own, private helicopter. The entire office and all field supervisors were invited to the wedding. The groom, Daiv was indeed a view of splendor but his heart was cold and wicked. Daiv was known to have a long term relationship with Ange. She was a very attractive and, yet, very naïve, young girl. She was blindly in love with Daiv, though, and did not realize that for years she was just being his toy. In the meantime, he was engaged to a rich girl, to fit his social standing. The guests at the reception seemed to be as cruel as Daiv. Ada could not believe what she was hearing. They expected Ange to jump out the wedding cake, naked? Was it appropriate to joke about Ange at that time? Poor girl was heartbroken. Have they had no heart?

Ange was supervising data entry staff. She was promoted to that position after Mr. Rose passed away. His death was so sudden that it came as a shock to everyone. There was nothing wrong with him until he went to see some Russian hypnotist, to stop smoking. Did the hypnosis do something to Mr. Rose? Ada remembered the day after he came back, smoke free. He got so emotional with Ada and Onie. Did he see something in them that they were not aware of? Ange and Onie have seen that same hypnotist and they both stopped smoking but they seemed to be alright. Everyone thought Ange and Onie were best friends and Ange confided in Onie, just as Ada did. Onie always seemed to be so sincere and innocent. Appearances often fool people, though, and that was so true about Onie. The entire office would soon know all about Ange's love life. Onie made sure she reported all the details to Daiv as well. As if that was not enough for Onie, she would always look for something to embarrass Ange, especially at lunch breaks. Ada remembered the day when Onie pointed at Ange and said: "Oh, I gave you that dress, didn't I?" Ange got very offended and answered: "No, you did not give it to me. I bought it from you because it was too small on you." Was Onie evil or what? Why would she want to humiliate Ange so much, and for what? Everyone in the office knew everything about her. Even Ada knew that both Ange and her sister were adopted because their mother could not have children, for she was handicapped.

Onie was an animal lover, though. She was never married and had no children, so she treated her cat like a baby. She also ran a campaign against animal cruelty and asked Ada if she would, too, sign the petition. Ada did that with a very heavy heart. What she would really want was to sign the petition against abortion. She was deeply troubled that she put animals' rights over humans'. A few years later she did get a chance to vote against abortions in her local parish but for now she thought she was doomed. Millions of unborn children were being slaughtered every day, and Onie would conveniently say that since abortion was such a controversial issue, she decided to write her term paper for school on menstruation subject. Every day as Ada drove to work, she saw a poster of a beautiful, newborn girl, in a fluffy white dress. The writing below the picture said: "Her right to live against the woman's right to choose". Ada's eyes were always tearful, when she looked at that poster.

Yet, there was a man in NEAT that always admired Ada and treated her with compassion. He was a foreigner, just like her. It just may be that his own experiences taught him to be kind to others. He soon perished too, just like Mr. Rose. With passing away of Eric Pashe things have changed drastically. The person that replaced Mr. Pashe was very obnoxious and had no respect for anyone. He was also prejudiced towards foreigners. Ada overheard that he had some health problems, too. She would tell herself: "You would think that someone that sick would have a human face and treat everyone with kindness." Onie got Ada in trouble with him. Mr. Love stopped by Ada's desk once inquiring why his company's account was past due. Ada was a very bad liar and when she was put on the spot she'd tell the truth. Onie disappeared quickly and as soon as Mr. Love left, Andy came by, fuming with anger. He told Ada that her job was in jeopardy because he heard from a reliable source that she defamed the company. Ada knew exactly what he was referring to and knew exactly who the reliable source was.

Then, Mr. Love was leaving. His company moved to California. There was a getaway party for him, in one of the dancing clubs. It was far away from Ada's work and she was afraid to drive on the highway. She had poor sense of direction and would never make it. Pete suggested to her that she could follow him. It sounded simple enough and Ada went along with the idea. However, in reality Ada found it very hard to follow him. It was dark outside and besides that she could not memorize the license plates, or the shape and color of Pete's car. A few times he had to pull over and wait for her. The trip seemed to have lasted forever. Ada did not even know how Pete managed not to lose her. It was not before long when Ada started to feel that she did not belong to that farewell party. She was slowly drinking her cola, while others were drinking alcoholic beverages, talking and laughing. She was never a talker. Her world was revolving around her family. However, she was afraid to talk about her children, for the fear that something would go wrong afterwards. She had countless good things to say about them but did not dare. She would not take that risk, to disrupt the peace of her family and dim the sunshine over her domain.

Mr. Love was very pleased to see Ada and since she was so quiet, he tried to have a conversation with her. Ada asked him how he liked his new home and how his family was. Then, she asked if his children went to see Disney World. At that Ada stopped. She got red on her face, trying to correct herself. "Wasn't Disney World on the other coast?" Mr. Love quickly said. "No, you are right Ada. California has its own Disney World, too. Ada felt very uncomfortable. When others would talk about actors, movies, TV shows and ball games, she was completely dumb in those things. She never had interest in them and as much as she would want to memorize the names of famous actors, she could not. It was useless. She could never remember the names or the faces. She stayed at the party for a little while, to be courteous but soon said goodbye to Mr. Love and proceeded to leave the place. However, her poor sense of direction left her wandering around the club. Finally, she asked a group of people: "Which way out?" They laughed profoundly at her. What Ada really meant was: "Can you please tell me where the exit door is?" But she often used incorrect phrases and was misunderstood, or even laughed at. Ada found her way out and when she got inside her car, she let go of her feelings. She cried all the way home.

Onie was upset because Bea put it in her head that when she would retire, Onie would take her place. When Rad came on board, with his accounting degree, it was obvious that he would eventually take Bea's place. Bea has been also teaching Onie that she needed to be tough, if she were to run the office. Onie followed her advice and she was very nasty to co-workers and vendors. Everyone in the office hated her. When Onie had no one to complain to, she would turn to Ada. She complained so much about Rad, mostly about his changing the way things were done in the office. She was not willing to accept any changes. She was being stubborn and refused to follow Rad's directions.

Then, one day Ada's children brought some posters from school and on one of them there was a kitty cat with eye glasses on. The writing on it said: "Too eager to play, too cute to study." Ada made a mistake of bringing that poster to work and giving it to Onie. She did not mean to be cruel to her. It was just one of Ada's metaphors. Ada forgot, however, that she was not in the position to make any jokes or any references that could be taken in two ways. She could not sleep that night. She could not stop thinking about the poster. Onie was old enough and experienced enough, to know the right from wrong. She did not need some double phrases, to remind her that if someone else was hired to run the business, with higher education, she was to accept it and have some respect. Ada's imagination was running wild that night. Was Onie going to be alright? Once, Onie told her co-workers a story, how her cat attacked her and left scratches all over her body. Moreover, Ada felt guilty, for she told Onie that Acil wanted her to have the poster. Why would she blame it on Acil? When Onie came to work the next day, everyone was concerned about her and was asking her how she was. Did everyone think that Ada would mean any harm to her? Anyway, everyone seemed to think that Ada had bad intentions giving that controversial poster to her.

In the days to come, Ada thought that she was being punished for that metaphorical poster she gave to Onie. She felt like her co-workers, and even some vendors she was dealing with, were playing her out. One day, a new computer technician came to the office to fix a computer problem. He surprised Ada by asking her if she was able to read and speak Polish language. Ada admitted that she did. He, then, asked her to translate something for him. He pulled out a handwritten letter. It seemed odd to Ada, because the man was of a dark skin. However, she quickly shrugged of that feeling, as she recalled that foreign students, especially those from poor African countries, were welcomed in Poland. It was very common to see students of different nationalities at the City of Warsaw. Ada had difficulty reading the handwriting, and even a harder time remembering what she was reading, not to mention translating it to English. The man told her that he just wanted to get the general idea what the letter was about. "General idea", Ada thought? After her breakdowns, she had a severe memory loss. She could not remember anything without writing it down first. Yes, she could probably translate the letter by writing it down and then, drawing the general idea. She was stuttering, trying to translate sentence after sentence. Rad came by, trying hard to cover up his laughter, as he looked at Ada. Onie was chuckling at her desk. Why did Ada agree to do that in the first place? Couldn't she simply refuse it? Why did she have to make a fool of herself?

There was, yet, another test that Ada was forced to undergo at NEAT. It was a math problem. It could be solved in two different ways. Ada was not feeling well and ignored some additional information that was given. Rad and Andy laughed at Ada, ridiculing her, when she gave them the answer. She explained to them that her answer was by averaging, because she failed to notice the extra information that was given. It was no use, though. Andy kept laughing, as he passed by Ada's desk and said: "There are two ways to skin the cat, right Ada?" As if that was not enough for him, he gave Ada some legal papers to review. They were from the Port Authority that the company was tied to. As Ada was reading, she was writing pencil notes, for her reference. Andy laughed in her face: "Oh yes, keep on going. Keep writing notes. Perhaps someone will recognize the handwriting". Ada also overheard Andy saying that he received a phone call from the landlord, stating that they need to put a stop to Ada's long hours, before she collapses. Ada thought to herself: "Can't anyone see that it is not the long hours that affect me but the psychological pressures that I am being subjected to?"

As Ada was struggling to keep her job, many members of her distant family passed away. First it was Aunt Fran's husband, then Uncle Mu and his wife He. When Ada was about to give birth to Esse, Fes' Aunt Hel died. Ada remembered going to her funeral. She felt great when she was carrying the baby in her womb. Her face seemed to be radiating with joy. At the reception, Auntie Sun and her sister Fran sat next to her. They talked during the whole time. Ada had a lot to say because she did not see them for some time. Aunt Fran wished Ada that she would have an easy and quick birth. Indeed, Ada gave birth to Esse that same night. Auntie Sun and Aunt Fran surprised Ada by visiting her at the hospital. They even brought her flowers. Ada had Esse on her bed and they marveled how beautiful and big she was. Indeed, she was very long and weighed over ten pounds. Before long, Aunt Fran suffered a stroke. She seemed to be alright, though, and, yet, her doctor said she needed the operation on her brain. Fran's daughter agreed to it. Ada regretted for not going to see Fran before her surgery. Needless to say, Aunt Fran never woke up after it and a day later, she passed away. Ada thought: "Why Aunt Fran's daughter agreed for her mother to have such a delicate surgery? If it wasn't for that, then, perhaps she would still be living."

Yet, most dramatic for Ada was Fes' Aunt Aria's death. Ben called Ada to let her know that she was comatose in the hospital. She seemed to be somewhat responsive, when he was telling her about Poland. She liked to hear the stories of that country. She used to always write to Fes' sister, Enie and send her packages. Ben asked Ada, if she would come to visit her in the hospital. He thought that if she spoke to her in her Polish language, perhaps Aunt Aria would wake up. Ada took his advice and kept talking, not only about Poland, but also how much she and Fes appreciated her friendship. She even visited them once, not caring that there was a war between them and Uncle Woo. Tears came out Aunt Aria's eyes, her feet twitched. She expired, right before Ada's eyes. When Ada was driving to the viewing the next night, she was thinking where she was going to park. To her surprise, there was a parking space right in a front of the funeral building, as if it was reserved for her. Ada was already emotionally distressed and could not stop crying and, yet, Uncle Woo kept talking to her. He did not seem to be mourning his sister's death at all. He wanted to know way too much about Acil! Ada's family lived in Kar then but Acil was finishing her school year in Eli. Ada told Uncle Woo that Acil did not like living in Kar. His response was: "Everyone likes to live where they are born." Ada was very much troubled that he was inquiring so much about Acil and had such a great grin on his face.

Ada did not want to miss work and, besides that, did not feel emotionally strong, so she did not go to Aunt Aria's funeral. She thought that going to the viewing and praying for her was enough. It was such a gloomy, dreary day. Ada was the first one in the office, so she set up the coffee makers, one with the regular coffee and one decaffeinated, as requested in the past by her bosses. Rad and Andy came in late, both at the same time. They were like ghostly appearances to Ada that came after her, to haunt her. Andy was saying things that were so familiar to her. "Did he know all about Aunt Aria's death?" Ada thought. "Why is he torturing me? I never did anything to him." But his words were like a whip to Ada. "What a mess!" He said. Ada had no clue what he was referring to. She asked: "What did I do now?" "Nothing", he said. "It's just the way you do things". Minutes later, she saw him coming out the kitchen, with Rad. They were both laughing, and the only words that Ada could catch were: "...Two alright, two coffees". Ada was getting more and more paranoid, but did not lose her head yet, and was not falling behind in her work. In fact, she was doing a great job.

There was a children's movie that was playing at that time, The Lion King. It was a cartoon movie about a lion cub that ran away from home, as guilt was implanted in him by a family member. That guilt drove him away from home to far away land, where he succeeded in getting rid of his guilt and lived rather peacefully. Ada perceived cartoons as metaphors to humans' feelings and expressions. Her homeland was once under oppression for many, many years. There was no freedom of speech, and all ideas were expressed as metaphors. In animal talks, often described in poems, there were hidden meanings that expressed the nation's struggle for independence. That's how Ada perceived animated movies in the new world. Each one of them had a hidden motto. Ada made a controversial statement to Onie, again using Acil. She stated that Acil felt that it was so cruel to implant guilty feelings in young child's mind. "That guilt, then, overwhelms the child and haunts him or her lifelong", Ada said. She was, in fact, referring to herself but was hiding behind Acil's cover, for fear of being further questioned.

After work that day, Ada stopped at one of the stores and bought the Lion King's animated movie, for her children. She was not herself anymore, though. She was paranoid and was thinking irrationally. Her heart was racing, as she was paying for the video. When she got home and none of her family was there, she was afraid that she would never see them again. She left the video on the table and lay down, trembling with fear. She did not know how long she was lying there, whispering the prayers. Finally, her family arrived and, then, she could not stop tears from coming down. It was a relief that her family was home and everything was fine.

As Ada was trying desperately to hold on to her job at NEAT, she was already losing touch with reality. When she drove by a train station, on her way from work one day, she thought she heard her sister, Akin crying: "Ada! I just saw

Ada!" She was petrified. Was it really true? Throughout her whole mental ordeal, she seemed to be having close encounters with her family members, as if the curtain dividing the continents was unveiling to her. She thought she was losing her mind. Would she dare abolish the proven theory that the earth was round and revolving around the sun? Could it be that the distance in time and land, was only a mere speculation? Could it be that her relatives were just a step away from her, separated from her by just an invisible wall?

Ada was so confused. Sometimes, she attributed all of her misfortunes to the Evil that she thought followed her everywhere. Other times, she thought she was dead and in hell. How else could she explain her feelings that everyone was reading her mind and knew everything about her? And, yet, at times, she felt as if she was experimented on and all her places of work were wired and bugged, and so were all the apartments she lived in and her house and telephones. "Why would anyone do that, though, for what purpose?" she thought. Ada was like a blindfolded woman, not recognizing anyone, trusting but at the same time suspicious of everyone. She was even suspicious of Fes. Would he be the one to give Ada away and allowing the bugs? Could he not see that it was destroying her life, her very existence? Ada recalled her, what seemed to be the last trip to the beach with Fes years ago. She had to use the bathroom and, as she was walking back to her blanket on the beach, Fes asked someone next to him: "What time is it?" Ada saw a flash of light. Did that person take a picture of her?

Part II

"Heavens and Earth are afire centuries long. Someone is leaving, for someone else to come back. Will I find in this wide world my second bank? Will someone be there waiting for me?" This song of the most famous singer of her country was sounding in Ada's ears. She once had the entire album of her songs. She was single then. She would write love letters to Fes abroad and send him love songs. She would sing along with that famous singer on the tape recordings. Ada was not young anymore, but the song was still very much alive in her. Her second bank now was in the unknown, on the River of Life. She knew that her days were counted. Sooner or later, she would have to face death, but she was not afraid. She was always a dreamer and often wondered what Paradise would be like. After all, Jesus himself spoke of it, when he was dying on the cross. When the crucified criminal next to him was asking him for forgiveness, Jesus looked at him, with love, and said to him: "I say to you, today you will be in Paradise with me". Jesus knew that he was sincere and truly sorry for all the crimes that he has committed. On another occasion, during his teaching, long before his crucifixion, Jesus spoke of that promised Paradise. "No ear has ever heard and no eye has ever seen what my father has prepared for his faithful servants". Ada could not help but to think: "Would she meet her dear father on that other bank? Would she meet her other departed relatives as well?"

Ada often thought that our Earth could very well be the Garden of Eden, if it was not for the Evil that always found its way in to disturb the beauty and tranquility of our planet. Ada wanted to believe that there was no Evil, as God would never allow that to happen to His creation. However, when she thought of all the crimes that were being committed every minute, all over the world, she could not be sure that the existence of evil forces could be eliminated. There were many dreamers before Ada, and most certainly many more were to come. Ada's dream of a perfect world drove her to madness. People like her were being cursed out from Church. It was Easter time, and Ada just came out from the hospital. She sought her escape in church. She was looking for the healing power of God. Instead she found the coldness and resentment from the priest. She thought that she was going to be walked out from that church or plainly speaking, thrown out. The mass was delayed for at least half an hour. The priest was refusing to come out to celebrate it. Ada was crying silently and was ready to walk out when he finally showed up. She knew that it was her former English teacher from high school that intervened on her behalf. She saw her speaking to him.

Despite her sickness, Ada did not want to part from church. She never missed a Sunday mass. That is how she was brought up. The medication was making her very drowsy, however, and she had trouble getting up in the morning. She woke up one Sunday, too late to go to the English mass but decided to go anyway, to join the Spanish mass at noon. She has been a regular church goer and could recite verse for verse the entire celebration of the Holy Mass. And so she did. As the people around her were praying in Spanish, she was silently saying the same in English. And then, the moment came that Ada dreaded ever since. After Mass, the congregation started reciting devotion prayers to Virgin Mary. As they did, they formed a circle by holding hands. Ada was pushed out the ring. She tried to get in but no one would let her in, no one would hold her hand. She left the church sobbing. Nothing could comfort her. She would be forever doomed. Then, it came fall and All Saints Day. Still, Ada was trying to hold on to the old customs. She went to see the priest and gave monetary offering for Holy Masses, one for her deceased father and one for her husband's. It was for a Spanish Mass because all English ones were already taken. When Ada attended the mass for her deceased father-in-law, she could not believe what she was seeing. That was not a Holy Mass at all. It was a play, a joke. The priest could not even pretend to be serious when he called out the name of the deceased. He laughed aloud. Ada did not walk out but she was sick to her stomach and very disturbed.

Slowly, Ada distanced herself from church. She discovered that she was much more at peace when she prayed silently at home, rather than in the house of God. Whatever happened to her, she had no control of it and hoped that she would be forgiven by our Lord, Jesus Christ. She often envisioned the story of Mary from Magdale who committed a sin for which, according to scriptures, she should have been stoned to death. Jesus saved her life, simply by saying to her accusers: "Let the one of you who never committed a sin cast the first stone." At that, they all slowly backed out, one by one, and disappeared. That story inspired Ada, for there was a ray of hope for her too. All of her life, she felt rejected and, in the later years, even despised. She hoped that one day she would find the eternal peace, the peace she so much longed for.

For Ada, everything was a constant struggle. She wanted very much to lock herself at home and never come out. Yet, she struggled to keep her sanity, for the sake of her children. They were the whole world for her. For years, Ada had to force herself to go to work or to do any chores outside her home. She avoided any social gatherings, not that she was anti-social, not at all. Ada had enough problems to deal with and did not need any additional stress. For the longest, doctors have been asking her if she heard voices. How could she explain the truth, though? She tried to isolate her mind from hearing anything. She heard voices but, to her, they seemed to be coming from outside. Mostly she heard them outside the wall of the room she was in. What was scaring her, though, was the fact that she could never see anyone, when she looked outside the window. Voices seemed to be so familiar to her sometimes. They sounded like the voices of her relatives abroad, just outside the wall. However, voices were not the only problem that Ada had to deal with. She kept seeing faces of her relatives, from the other continent.

The most dramatic encounter for Ada was with her deceased father. Ada was driving to work, trying to hold on to it, despite the fact that she was being on the verge of nervous breakdown. She passed by a little shopping center on Broad Street. On the corner, there was a bus stop and, as Ada looked to the left, in the crowd she saw her father standing. He looked just as she has last seen him, during the family re-union in 1981, when Acil was only one year old. He was even wearing the same clothes. Ada was so sorry she did not stop the car in the middle of the street and jump out, to get the closer look. Was it really her father? Would she be able to touch him, to hold him? Would she be able to take him home with her? Ada would never know. She was scared to turn back. What was the meaning of that apparition? Was her father trying to reassure her that he was around, watching over her? Was he trying to tell her that she was not walking alone through her life, for he was always with her? Ada was not well at all, though. She felt like she has been caught between two worlds, and she was paranoid. After the vision of her father, she feared that she would not be able to find her children and her husband at home.

Ada thought she has seen other members of her family, too, but those were all living relatives abroad. Shortly after the encounter with her father, she saw her mother, in front of the drug store, across the street from the apartment building they used to live. Her mother lived with them there, when she visited them, before Esse was born. Again, Ada could not have been mistaken. Her mother looked exactly like she did when she was leaving back home. She was wearing her burgundy coat, with matching pocket book that she bought in Eli. As Ada passed by, she wanted to turn back and run to her but was afraid that it would be no return, and she would never find her children. Ada lived in constant fear that her children and her husband would disappear. Staying at home, when she lost her job, did not help her a bit. She was afraid to lose the sight of her children, when they were leaving for school. All day long, she was tormented by fear that they might not come back home. One day, in the snowy weather, Ada was driving to pick up Anon and Esse from school. Suddenly, she thought she saw her younger brother, Acie standing on the sidewalk. She was all shook up. As soon as she got home, she picked up the phone and called him.

Acie had no idea what Ada has been going through, though. He sounded well and happy. His first words were not "How are you?", but "You got a lot of snow, didn't you?" Ada was in shock and had difficulty speaking, so she just listened to Acie rattling about this and that. Through the whole time, tears were running down her face. She was motionless, her face felt numb, and she felt dead inside. However, she would not let her brother sense that anything was wrong. After all, what could her brothers and sisters do for her? Ada already made one mistake in the past, by calling her sister, Tila when she could not control her anxieties. She was at the post office, to buy some postage stamps. On her way home, she saw a huge, white trailer with the words "Camping" written on it. A crowd of people exited the trailer onto the sidewalk. One of them looked just like her Aunt Fia, from her old country. Those people were not happy at all. In fact, they looked very angry and seemed to be pushed around. Ada almost ran home. She was even more scared when she saw the telephone company doing something to the wires, by her home. She could not help herself. She desperately needed to speak to someone. She was able to reach her sister, Tila on the telephone and described her experiences to her. Tila sympathized with her and tried to find the reasonable explanation for what Ada described to her. Ada was petrified that her relatives were captured and trapped in that white, "Camping" van. After speaking to Tila, she was a little relieved because everything seemed to be fine there.

Other apparitions that Ada encountered were her sisters, Mar and Ria and her brother, Mare. Were those visions for real? Or, was it just Ada's imagination? Sometimes, Ada even had a difficulty to tell whether she was asleep or awake.

Nights were just as much tormenting for Ada as her daily struggles. She has been experiencing a phenomenon that she could not explain. Was it a dream? Was it a near death experience? She would often find herself paralyzed. Her eyes seemed to be opened and she was staring in a familiar spot of the room. She could not move, though, or turn her eyes. It felt like she was glued to bed. Something seemed to be overcoming her body. She felt freezing cold. In her mind she was whispering a prayer or sometimes even cry: "Leave me alone! Go away!" Some nightmares did not make sense to her and most of them she was happy not to remember. Yet, others seemed to be so vivid and real to her. One of such nightmares lasted all night long. Ada was running away with her infant grandson. It seemed, as if she was trying to hide him, to protect him. She could run no more, for she tripped and fell. She could not get up but was still holding on to the baby. She was dragging herself on her knees, supporting the baby in her arms by her elbows. She has been hearing weird sounds. A few times, she seemed to have awakened and saw the surroundings of the room, only to slip back to that same nightmare.

Lener was a very quiet, easy going baby. As soon as he started walking though, the trouble started. He would get everywhere. He could not be left alone for a minute. Ada and Acil learned that pretty soon. He was just about walking, when he snuck outside the house, onto the street. Ada and Acil ran outside, as they heard cars outside blowing the horns. Then, they saw him; they saw Lener in the middle of the street, between cars. Ada's heart stopped, as Acil ran and grabbed her son. It was a miracle that nothing has happened to him. Could it be that Ada's father whom she met at the crossroads was watching over her family? Another incident was just as dramatic. Ada ran upstairs, as someone whispered to her that Lener was on the roof. People were standing outside, motionless and speechless, looking up at the baby on the steep roof, outside the window on the second floor. Everyone lost their heads. No one knew what to do and feared the worst. Anon did not lose his head, though. As quickly and silently as a wild cat, he ran to the second floor, climbed outside the window, and grabbed Lener. Everyone relaxed, then, and Ada was crying, the tears of joy that her grandson was safe.

As much as Ada wanted to stay home and babysit Lener, when he was born, her financial situation did not allow it. So, she found a new job and stayed with Mr. Occom's company for nine and half years. She loved her work, though. It kept her mind occupied. It was a very fast paced office. Some days, Ada had to do multiple tasks, at the same time. She worked very long hours, too. Even though she was supposed to be a supervisor, many times she ended up doing most of the work by herself. She was getting a decent salary that was envied by her co-workers but the hours that she had to work were outweighing by far that compensation. Yet, Ada was happy that she could go to work every day, like a normal citizen. It was very important to her, especially when her children reached the adolescence age. For once, she felt that they did not have to feel embarrassed by their mother. It was not easy, however. Every now and then, the "Silver Shadow" would catch up with Ada and keep her tormented for months. Ada once read a book, "Silver Shadow", about the evil, marked by the silver shadow that could find its prey everywhere. There was no hiding place from it.

"Silver Shadow" caught up with Ada, after working only for one year for Mr. Occom. One year of normal life, in the new surroundings and, once again, Ada's peace of mind was gone forever. She felt so much anxiety inside of her that she wished to be dead. Did it have anything to do with wiring of the office building? She thought. During her first year, when they had the office downstairs, in the old trailer, she was fine but there were no cameras there. She felt very anxious, though, every time she had to go to the nursing home, next door. Ada never refused to go, when her boss, Asu asked her. However, it was a torture for her. It was like walking into the flames of Gehena. It felt like slipping through an invisible wall, into the burning fires of hell. Ada would recognize maybe a couple of faces, or at least the director's face. They all seemed to be unreal, though, almost like floating in the air. They grinned at her, sending chills all over her body. After each trip, Ada would sit at her desk, desperately trying to stop tears pouring down her face.

Things were only to get worse for her, though, after her office was wired and there were cameras all over the place. Asu, however, always had the way of calming her down. She was very strong, strict, and demanding with work but at the same time she was so gentle and understanding. Ada's heart was breaking, when she heard her other boss, Zuza spreading ugly rumors about Asu, criticizing her work, and making her look bad in the owner's eyes. Then, the day came that Asu announced that she was resigning. Ada knew that Asu had personal problems at home. Zuza spread the gossips about it months ago. Asu told Ada that she wanted to start her life anew, and leave all of her problems behind. Ada was a little shaken. She was losing not only a great boss but also a true friend.

Asu was a great teacher and she was very much computer oriented. Ada finally learned from her how to do spreadsheets on the computer. She could not believe how simple it was. Obviously her previous bosses, Je and Rad played her out and did not really want her to learn it. Ada praised Asu for being such a great teacher and Asu praised Ada for being such a great student. Asu was not afraid to delegate a lot of things that she was doing to Ada. She was mastering new things very quickly. Overall, Asu gave Ada a very strong accounting foundation. It was a tearful goodbye, then, when Asu was leaving.

Things changed drastically in the office when Asu left. Zuza had the new financial director, Don wrapped around her fingers and was taking total control of Mr. Occom's businesses. Mr. Occom trusted her blindly. When Asu was gone, Zuza found someone else to pick on. She feared Ada, thinking of her as the rival, especially because Ada's daughter, Acil was working in the same office. Zuza was trying everything to make Ada's life miserable. It came to the point that Ada could not take that any longer and handed in her resignation note. She thought that in two weeks she might be able to find something. And she did, she found a new job. Not exactly what she wanted, but something to get away from Zuza. Zuza was thrilled that Ada was leaving. She wanted her out as soon as possible. She did not want anything to come in the way, so she came to Ada, trying to convince her to use her benefit hours, instead of working those last two weeks.

Zuza's devious way of getting rid of Ada got complicated, however, when Nat found out about Ada's resignation. Zuza made a mistake of sending Ada's resignation letter to the business office, to be filed in her personnel file. Nat, business director valued Ada's work and, when she read her resignation note, she was very angry with Zuza. Ada remembered that day. Her desk was facing Zuza's. The phone rang and Zuza turned bright red, when she was talking on the phone. In a little while, Zuza came to Ada's desk, with her tune changed. Now, she was trying to convince Ada to stay, pointing out all the good things about the company. She offered Ada higher salary and, needless to say, Ada decided to stay. She regretted it very much, later on, but what was done was done.

Ada was always very generous. Her financial situation was not good and she always struggled from pay to pay. Yet, she would always try to help someone in need or to do something nice for someone. Those gestures usually backfired at her. It was no different at Monmouth. Ada felt sorry for her co-worker whose husband passed away. Bela just paid for her husband's funeral expenses and there she was, being pressured by Zuza to pay back the money she owed to the company. Ada found out that the company sponsored Bela and she had to pay back for all the associated with it expenses. Ada felt sorry for her and gave her the money she needed for Zuza. Would you know? Bela no longer was that sweet, always willing to help girl. Moreover, she passed around jokes that were like a bullet hitting Ada's heart. One day, she asked Ada, laughing: "Do you have change for forty dollars?" Ada was angry and wanted to say to her: "I have, at forty years, I became a grandmother." Ada was as sensitive to the word "forty" as to the words "two", "chips", and a "copy", as if they were all riddles to a puzzle. She almost lost her life years ago on account of forty dollars. Then, when her son, Anon was born, the neighbor gave forty dollars to her, as a gift to welcome the new baby. Ada tried to stop her mind from analyzing everything that has been said to her, but was not too successful. She was even afraid to use a copy machine at work, for the murmurs around her: "Make more copies" seemed unbearable to her.

Why was Ada so scared of "Make more copies" phrases? Well, it went back to her fourth breakdown, when Acil was pregnant. Esse was only six years old. It was late at night and everyone was sleeping, everyone except Ada.

Suddenly Esse woke up and went around, checking if all the doors were locked. Then, she looked at Ada and said: "Don't worry, we can make more copies." Ada was petrified. What has gotten into her daughter? Surely, it was not her six year old speaking to her in that fashion? Trembling, she embraced her daughter, picked her up, kissed her, and put her in bed.

Bela was not the only one that changed her colors after Ada's good gesture. Don changed as well, after a surprise birthday gift from Ada. She found out about it at the end of that day and felt bad that no one did anything for him. When she got home, she called the florist and ordered flowers to be delivered to him. She did not want him to know that the flowers were from her, so she asked if the card could read: "Happy Birthday, from the Office Staff". The next day, Don was going crazy, trying to find out who did it. Zuza, somehow, knew that it was Ada. She came up to her and asked how much she paid for the flowers, so she could reimburse her from the office petty cash. Zuza also made the arrangements for the luncheon. Don was choked up when he gave a brief speech during the luncheon. It was the first time in his life that someone would send him flowers. Ada paid for that deed plentiful. Once again, the invisible wall sealing the past opened up. Everyone around her was murmuring. She also kept hearing angry voices and evil laughter. Was her new boss, Alan part of the play? Ada turned around, when she heard him on the phone: "Have you heard the latest brainstorm that we are in hell?" He was laughing hysterically. At least he was still kind to Ada, though, and did not seem to be changed. Everyone else did, especially Don. He acted so cruel to Ada and he did not look like himself. He looked like he was electrified or "possessed". Ada was heartbroken when he was picking on her. "What did I ever do to him?" She thought. Other co-workers seemed to have changed as well. "...No, thank you. What am I going to feed my children, clouds?" Ive said. Those words pierced Ada right in her heart. Was it not that one of the verses of her morning anthem to Virgin Mary went: "Oh Maria, thou art on the highest, and throne of yours is in the pillar of clouds"? Ada, who always used similes and metaphors, knew that the phrase mentioned was just a figure of speech. How did Ive know that verse though? Was she, too, reading Ada's mind?

Zuza seemed to be playing as well. As she was suddenly leaving the office, Anti would say: "Bye, mom. Take care". She would answer: "I'll be back!" Ada did not know what was going on. She, too, wasn't herself and had a very hard time concentrating on her work. Sometimes, she felt so sore inside that she was hardly getting any work done but was afraid to go home. No, she would not let her co-workers know that something was wrong with her. That would make her work impossible, just like on her previous jobs. Then, it was Ash Wednesday and Don invited a priest to stop at the office, to give ashes. Ada heard Don say: "Perhaps, this will help." "Was he referring to me?" Ada thought. Anyway, when the priest arrived and Ada's co-workers were lining up to get ashes, Ada went to the ladies room. She locked the door and turned off the lights. She always had the feeling that she was being spied on, even in the bathroom. In the darkness of the room Ada made the sign of the cross on her forehead and said: "Ashes to ashes. Dust to dust." The meaning of it was that her human body was nothing but the dust and to dust it was to return someday, when her earthly journey would be over and her destiny fulfilled.

Ada tried to focus only on the work that she had to do and block her mind from everything else that has been going on around her. It was hard to concentrate, though, with everyone around her acting up. It was so unreal, almost like a perfect play. One day, when Ada could no longer take Don's sarcasm and was about to break, Alan came over to her and with his soft voice asked for something. At that Ada's eyes turned misty, as she whispered in her mind: "I can work with you." That was like a magic phrase. It brought everything back to the way it used to be.

During Ada's years at Monmouth, she also went through the traumatic experience of her husband's car accident that he merely survived. In cases like that, Ada always found the strength and was able to put all of her own problems aside and turn all of her attention and devotion to the one in need. After he got well, Fes would always say that if it wasn't for Ada's support he would never have gotten better, or even worse, he would not have survived the accident. As for her, she was so lonely, though. She had not even one friend to turn to.

Why did Ada have such a difficulty making friends? The closest friend she has ever had was Ali years ago. She would forever be grateful to her for coming to her rescue, when she had to run away from Uncle Woo because he threatened to kill her. She not only took her to her house but also helped her to find an apartment. For that reason, she pleaded on Ali's behalf, to get her a job. She knew Fes' boss only a little from a few times she spoke to him and, yet, she was bold enough to ask for a job for her. Ali did not associate much with Ada, though, because she caught her kissing her husband. Little did Ali know that on the part of Ada it was just an innocent kiss on a cheek, thanking him for his and Ali's hospitality and allowing her to stay at their house when she had nowhere to go?

Ada did understand Ali's fears, however. She heard the tearful tale of her life. Stan married Ali and, then, brought her to America. He had his whole family here, whereas, Ali was all alone, totally dependent on Stan. She was very pretty and was always wearing makeup, making her beautiful face features even more visible. It was not before long that Stan's father began making advances at poor Ali. She resisted and threatened him that she would tell her husband. Stan's father beat her to it, however. Of course everything that he told Stan was a lie. He made accusations that Ali was cheating on him. Ali could not defend herself, as Stan did not want to hear her part of the story. He threatened to leave her. Ali got on her knees, then, begging him for forgiveness. She was able to sweeten him up and make him stay. They managed to have four children. The last two were twins. Ali was very worried about them because they were about two years old and did not speak yet. What worried Ali even more was the fact that the two boys communicated with each other perfectly, in the language not known to anyone.

What made Ada give a kiss to Ali's husband that one night, when she was leaving their house? She always felt that she did a great injustice to her friend, Ali. Why did she have to tell Auntie Sun about her friend's hardships, too? It was like giving Uncle Woo, yet, another prey. Helping Ali to get a job could not compensate for the damage done to her. Ali, just like Ada, suffered from depression. Her yolk got even heavier when Stan left her. She struggled to keep her job but finally had to let go. No one knew what happened to her. It broke Ada's heart when, years later, Fes found an article about her in Obituaries section. She was caring for an elderly person, when she suffered a heart attack and died. Ada thought she may have been doing that work ever since she lost her job. She said goodbye to her in her prayers. "Ali's journey ended and finally she was free and at peace", Ada thought. Tearfully she would say to Ali in her thoughts: "Nothing can hurt you now. You feel no pain; you need not to shed any more tears."

Ada first met Ali at Polish Saturday school, teaching her native language. However, Ada did not last long at that school. She was a good tutor but not a classroom teacher. Standing up in front of the class was making her dizzy. At times, she felt as if she was losing control and was going to faint any moment. Yet, she managed to hang on for a few months. That's how she got to know a young priest that came from her native country. He was not only young but also very energetic and, in a sense, a dreamer. He was creative, too, and came up with a modern version of Christmas Pageant. Everyone from Polish Saturday School had a part in it. Ada got a leading role of Virgin Mary. At the time Ada made her reconciliation with Auntie Sun and Uncle Woo, so her aunt asked their neighbor, who was a seamstress, to sew Virgin Mary's costume for her.

Ada's part in the pageant was breathtaking, even though she did not sing a solo that Father Kazi originally proposed. Ada should have sung it, though. She was a good singer and it would have been so appropriate for her role to sing: "Lullaby, little Jesus, my sweetest pearl. Lullaby, my favorite delight. Lullaby, my little Jesus, lullaby and thou, Holy Mother bring comfort to him and wipe of his tears". However, it was beautiful, when the whole chorus of little children sang that lullaby.

It did not take long for Father Kazi to realize that something was wrong at Ada's house. Auntie Sun kept inviting him to her house, since she felt sorry for him that he had no family in America. Each visit made Uncle Woo only so much angrier. Ada felt comfortable with Father Kazi around and was eager to serve him, even if it was only a glass of water. Uncle Woo's displeasure could not escape Father Kazi's attention. He approached Ada once, asking her frankly if Uncle Woo's behavior was directed particularly at him or was it common to all visitors in the house. Ada was afraid to make any confessions, so she quickly said that it had nothing to do with him.

It was summertime. Ada called out sick from work, when Auntie Sun and Uncle Woo decided to take Father Kazi on a boat ride in New York. They all took a bus to the city. Father Kazi truly admired it. They only had a few blocks to walk to the pier, to take the boat. There, Ada had a chance to talk more to Father Kazi but that was no time or place for confessions, even though she made a statement that her sick callout was not quite a lie because she needed time off for her mental health. Eventually, Father Kazi found out about Uncle Woo's advances at Ada but did nothing about it. It was just before their wedding when Fes told him about it. Ada also remembered getting from him, as a wedding present, an oriental style miniature tea set. That was not what Ada needed, though. She was a nervous wreck. She was a walking shadow of death. She had no one to talk to, no one to comfort her. Did not Father Kazi see that she needed him more than ever? As a priest, should he not have a role of a counselor? He quickly disappeared from Ada's life and she would never see him again.

Even though, after her marriage, Ada did not associate with the Polish School anymore, she heard that Father Kazi held another Christmas Pageant, yet. This time Ada's "friend", Hana was playing the role of the Virgin Mary. Hana took Ada's place at Auntie Sun's and Uncle Woo's house, as Ada learned. "How could she"? Ada thought. "I confided in her, telling her what I have been through over there!" Hana's aunt had a very sick husband and everyone knew that he was slowly dying. Even though Hana was just visiting her aunt, she had secret dreams of staying in America. "Was she that desperate to stay, though, that she took my place in that snake pit?" Ada thought. She would never see Hana after her wedding and often wondered: "Did Uncle Woo change, to prove that I was wrong and everything was nothing but my own imagination, as they said"? Hana lived with Auntie Sun and Uncle Woo until she got her papers. One of Auntie Sun's friends, a doctor signed sponsorship papers for her. On what terms did Hana leave Auntie Sun and Uncle Woo's house? Ada would never know. She learned, however, that Bie took Hana's place there.

Bie was Ada's high school friend, in her native country of Poland. She seemed to be very excited about Ada going to America. She wanted to help her in every way she could. She accompanied her to the city hall, to get her passport. A few times she invited her to spend the night over her house. Bie was so little, compared to Ada. Ada could not understand why she was so short, for her parents were of a normal height. When Ada left for America, Bie kept in touch by writing frequent letters. "Did Bie get that picture of me, with my breasts exposed, that Auntie Sun vouched to send to everyone?" Ada could not help but to think. Apparently, Auntie Sun, once more, made the arrangements with her niece, Ver to correspond with Bie, just as she did with Ada years ago. Then, they invited her to come to America. Bie even came to visit Ada in her apartment at Court Gubor. However, things were not the same anymore. "What did she come for, anyway? Was it just a pure curiosity how I was managing?" Ada wondered. Bie's visit with Auntie Sun and Uncle Woo has been extended to almost a year, or longer, because of the political unrest in her native country. Ada ran into her in the mini shopping mall. Ada had her little Acil with her. She must have been about three years old then. One quick moment of Ada's concentration on something else and Acil was gone. Ada was running around the store like a crazy woman. Her knees were weak, her heart was pounding, and her face was covered with a cold sweat. She felt like she was dying. At that she noticed Auntie Sun and Bie but they did not seem to see her. One closer look, and Ada realized that they seemed to be somewhat transformed. They did not seem real. It was all like a different world. Did Ada just encounter Auntie Sun's and Bie's ghostly apparitions? Or was it once again just Ada's wild imagination, out of fear for her daughter? Finally, Ada found Acil and she could not stop hugging and kissing her. Her face was wet from tears but she felt relieved.

Ada would often tell herself: "Put the past behind you." Yet, as her journey continued, she could not separate the past and the present. She often wondered off and made no sense at times. Her commingling of two worlds, the past and the present, and her inability to put the past behind her attributed to her mental anguish. Would the past forever haunt her and keep her prisoner in her four walls? Everything seemed to be indicating that. After more than two decades, Ada finally stopped feeling guilty over Yas, Acil's friend. When Ada's family was living in the City of Kar, Yas ran away from home and came to Ada's house. Shortly after, Yas' mother called and threatened that she was going to bring police over there, as it was illegal to hide runaways. Yas was petrified that she would be sent back home. As Ada listened to Yas' story over and over again, she concluded that there was something more to that than what she has heard. She knew that Yas was telling the truth and, yet, her story did not make sense. Why would Yas' mother's boyfriend be spying on her and make such a big issue about catching her kissing a boy? Yas was fourteen years old and she was a sensible girl, knowing the right from wrong. Did her mother have the right to beat her up? What mother would do that to her child? As there were too many unanswered questions and Ada did not know what to do, she advised Yas to call DYFS. She supported Yas' story when the investigator came to the house. Poor Ada, she felt so sick that she has done a horrible thing. Acil comforted her later by telling her the truth about Yas. For the longest time Yas' grandmother had custody of her. There has been evidence of prior abuse and that's why Yas' mother had no rights to her. "She wanted to keep her against her will, then, and illegally?" Ada thought. "Silver shadow" consumed Ada, however, and she saw herself drowning deeper and deeper. Was it Yas' mother's curse, or just a pure coincidence? She was dying, once again, this time for Yas. Once again, she had no control of her life and her feelings.

As much as Ada wanted to erase from her memory, the family's two years in the City of Kar, she found it impossible. That was the worst time of her life. That small Portuguese community was not at all sympathetic to her. The family problems were soon to be known to the entire community. Ada, as weak as she was, was trying to patch things up but for how long? She did not have a single friend. At the end, she suffered her fourth nervous breakdown. She was thankful, though, that her daughter, Acil was spared the mental anguish that she had to undergo. She feared so much for her.

Part III

"I'm walking the path of life. One of which, day by day is getting tougher, as years go by. You brought me here, into this big, hard world as your little girl; daddy's little girl. Mistakes I've made but I've learned a lot. And, although I'm older, I still love you, and I hope you still consider me your little girl. I'm walking the path of life. It's hard, but I'm still walking. I just hope I don't have to walk alone." Ada was all in tears, reading this poem that Acil once wrote as a teenager. She found it in the basement with lots of other things that Acil accumulated. It was such an emotional poem and Ada was deeply moved by it. She kept whispering to herself: "No, my child. You will never walk alone for I will always be there for you and your children. She loved Acil so much. She deserved so much more than what she had, after everything she has been through. When the scriptures said about purification time: "Woe to the mothers who at that time find themselves carrying a child in the womb", it seemed to be so true. There was no better way to describe everything that Acil has been subjected to when she was pregnant with Lener. At first, it was her own father that she had to face and who not only practically disowned her but even tried to hurt her, and Anon had to come to her rescue and, subsequently, Ada who at that point wrote the death warrant on Fes, if there was no other way to stop him from hurting her two children. Then, she was subjected to some sort of psychological torment and developed schizophrenic-like symptoms, mostly paranoia of being watched and fears that something was about to happen to her and the baby. She even believed that the neighbors in the apartment downstairs were doing voodoo on her. However, she survived that trial and was able to overcome her temporary anxiety. Instead, she suffered nine, long months of psychological and physical abuse from her baby's father. He wanted to have the total control of her and did everything to satisfy his selfish ego. She suffered so much abuse from him that it was even a miracle that she survived the pregnancy and gave birth to a beautiful baby boy, Lener. Ada's brother, Anon who witnessed all that was skeptical of ever wanting children of his own.

The experiences that Acil went through while pregnant with Lener made her not wanting to let anyone know when she conceived Asti. She went through entire nine months without anyone suspecting anything. It was not too difficult, though, because at that time the baggy clothes were very much in style. She was also in self denial and thought of it as not true, as something that would eventually go away. She was very scared, then, when the birth time came and ended up at Saint Michael's hospital. She made a very good decision, though, of keeping her baby, despite social workers' suggestions of giving up her daughter for adoption. Ada was full of admiration for her, when she found out about all that from Anon. She was in tears when she first saw Asti in the apartment that Acil shared with her spouse. She was such a beautiful baby and Ada thought she looked just like her mom. Acil also told her a story of Lener's reaction to his baby sister. When she lay Asti down on the bed and called Lener to come to see his sister, he stood motionless for a second and then ran up to her and smacked her on the face. Acil knew he did not mean it, for right after that he broke out in tears. She, then, sat him on her lap and embraced him, assuring him that Asti will never take his place in her heart, for she loved both of them.

Acil tried everything to make her relationship with her spouse work. They rented an apartment together and she was able to put up with him for quite a few years. However, it came to the point that she feared not only for her own safety but also her children's and moved in with Ada. When her children got older, they reached the ultimate decision that they did not want anything to do with their father. However, after long separation, Asti still had a heart to invite her father to her Sweet Sixteen Birthday Party and had her dance with him. It was so heart breaking for Ada. There was no spark of emotion in his eyes, as if he were dead. She felt so bad for Asti. She so much wanted to have a father in her life but she discovered that night that that man whom she called a father was a complete stranger to her. She could not believe what she was seeing. There was not even a trace of humanity in his face. He looked just like a Zombie. Ada could not help but to think: "Is that what the drugs did to him?"

As much as Ada loved her grandchildren she never bragged about them. She was afraid that if she did they would change. Lener was a very good singer. He had a beautiful voice and Ada hoped that one day someone would discover him and make him a singer. She thought he took it after her. She always loved to sing when she was young and free. "Or, perhaps he took it after my mother?" Ada thought, as she recalled her mother's successful recording of the folklore singing in "Kamionczanki" group. In many ways Lener reminded Ada of her grandfather, too. She loved to listen to his grandfather's tales when she was a little girl. He talked so much wisdom and common sense. Lener was so much like him. He loved science and could give Ada a lengthy speech on any given subject.

Asti was so much like her mother. She even looked like her, except for her hazel eyes. Asti loved to dance, model, and act. At the age of ten she participated in pre-teen miss contest. Esse was her sponsor and manager. For Asti it was the experience of her life. She enjoyed it very much. She had no problem associating with all those rich, pampered girls participating in the contest. Even though Asti did not win, she got the taste of the rich people's life. She found out, though, that she was much better off being her own plain self than all that make believe, fairy world.

Ada was very pleased and content to see that her children and grandchildren had so much confidence in themselves and were not afraid of anything. They were just the opposite of her, except for having her warm, affectionate personality. Ada was also pleased that Acil had one friend that she could always rely on. Yas was always there for her. She was a true friend through the years. Even though Yas had a very difficult childhood and teenage years, she was able to overcome it all. She became strong, secure, and confident of herself as years went by. It was heartbreaking to the entire Ada's family when she died from cancer, leaving two little children behind. If one talks about Irony of Life, Yas becomes a symbol of it. All the abuse: sexual, physical, psychological and emotional that she suffered as a little girl and a teenager made her adult life impossible to endure because she would never trust a man or respect him. When everything seemed to be working out for her, for she got married and bought a house and then gave birth to twins: a girl and a boy, thus starting a family, it all soon backfired at her. She started having marital problems and she blamed herself for it, due to the mood swings she was suffering. It was killing her when her husband fell for another woman. She was spared the agony of going through the divorce when she died but who would ever replace her in her children's lives?

Part IV

"I am suffering, slipping in and out of consciousness. I don't see those white frocks anymore; do not hear my brothers screaming from pain. I see pictures spinning in my mind; I reminisce the past. I see the face of Death but I do not fear. After all those days of suffering, I am all at ease. I feel so light and content. I am completely free." Ada was sobbing while she was reading this poem that her sister Ria wrote after their father's death. Ada was far away, on another continent when her father was suffering before his death. She was not there to comfort him, for him to feel her presence. She knew she was forgiven, though, and she was grateful to her brothers and sisters for being there for her father. Over the years Ada accumulated lots of letters and other valuables from her home country. As she got old, everything was even more precious to her. She found telegrams from her family abroad about her father's critical condition. How much she would want to bring those days back! She should have been there, by her father's side, holding and comforting him.

With her eyes tearful, Ada reached for another piece of paper, with Ria's poems. "His face became wrinkled; his hands more and more shaky. His eyesight became of that of a newborn child. And his speech grew more and more difficult. He no longer had the strength to pull himself off the bed or to call out for help. What was left was a long waiting period; for someone dear to stand by his side, dear and, yet, not known. His face lit up somewhat each time a gentle hand picked up his head. Could he feel or taste the food in his mouth? He would embrace the hand of the stranger. There were no words of thank you, no smile on his suffering face; only that dramatic and unforgotten hand grip." Ada loved her father so much and often blamed herself for his death. She thought that if she would not have left her father's house, things may have been different. Could she ever put the past behind her and live with the present?

Ada remembered the priest's preaching at one of the Sunday's masses. She was not quite well. What was that preaching about? Was it not one of the proverbs from the New Testament? Was it not about the son that took his father's inheritance and blew it all up, feasting and loose living? Why would Ada feel that the priest was talking directly to her? His words were scourging her soul and piercing her heart. When she left that church, the words were still sounding in her mind: "He was waiting and waiting for her son to return home! With each knock on the door, his face would light up; but it was not him." Why were those words like a whip on her body? She was sure her father has been waiting for her, on the bed of death, to say the last goodbye. Ada herself was only half alive, though, and was it not that her family said goodbye to her when she was only eighteen years of age?

Everyone envied Ada when she was leaving for America. They knew that she would never come back. Ada did visit, though, with Fes and Acil who was only one year old at that time. She was able to enjoy her father, once again, before he got seriously ill in a few months that followed. She unveiled the curtain dividing the continents and abolished the myth of the paradise land or the land of no return. It was a joyous re-union and Ada was sure that her father had that picture in his mind when his mortal life was fulfilled. Ada was so eager to do things with him when she visited! She was even ready to milk the cows or clean the manure in the stable. However, her father was not doing those things anymore. Ada's brothers and sisters were taking care of everything. It was not the best time for Ada to travel with little Acil, though. It was a late fall and in Ada's village there was a big snow storm and it was extremely cold. Even though Ada was dressing Acil very warm, it did not take long for her to catch a cold. Ada had her hands full then. Her whole world revolved around Acil and she could not enjoy her family anymore, especially when Acil was running a high temperature. Ada was always afraid of high fevers in children. She could never forget her infant brother Mare taking convulsions from it. And then, once again, after a week spent with her family, there was a tearful goodbye. Ada was happy, though. Her family did alright. She could not happen to notice some new improvements to the house. Her brother, Acie who was a carpenter made some kitchen cabinets and Mare did the plumbing in the house. They had a bathroom inside, with the toilet, sink, and the tub. They even had hot water.

Ada would go back to her home country again and again, no matter what the costs were. She wanted to keep ties with her brothers and sisters and, especially, with her mother. It was not easy for Ada's mother to raise her young children by herself. At the time when Ada's father passed away Akin was only sixteen and Tila was seventeen. Nineteen-year old Acie took his father's death very hard. He was running home from work to say the last goodbye to his father but he did not make it. He was in a depressive state for a long time and did not get over it until he met his wife, Bea. It was then that he found a new meaning to his life and found it worthwhile.

Overall, Ada has been back to her own country six times and expected many more to come. She recorded movies on some of those trips, including her first family re-union. Ada wished that the movies from her first trip to Poland had a sound to it. Wouldn't it be wonderful for Ada to hear her father's voice? Fortunately, she did have his father's voice saved. It was on the tape recording from All Saints Day and Christmas of 1975 that her family sent her to the United States.

Some of Ada's family members visited her in United States as well. Besides Mar with her daughter and Ada's mother, after a long interval, Ada's brother Mare came to

United States. Ada greatly enjoyed her family members' visits. She tried to make their stay as pleasurable as she could. No one knew, however, that each visit was a tremendous strain on her. Was it a curse that she could not enjoy her relatives visit? Instead of happiness she would experience the paranoia and great anxiety.

Ada would never complain about anything. Did keeping things to herself contribute to her breakdowns? Perhaps, it did but there was much more to it. Everything was always on her shoulders. She had to cope with her affliction and at the same time take care of her family. She was always afraid to lose control, in fear that her family would be left without a roof over their heads and no food to eat. She needed emotional support so bad and instead she had to provide it to her growing children and to her husband. Ada has always been very weak, physically and emotionally. She always pushed herself to the limits. Whatever she did it was taking the last bit of her strength to complete it. Every time she exerted herself physically, she paid for it emotionally in days to come. Ada could take a lot of pain, though, and would never give up. She was more afraid of psychological pressures that caused her anxieties and paranoia. However, no one could help her with that, not even her brothers and sisters.

Ada remembered that at the toughest times of her life Acie suggested that she would come back to her home country. He offered to share his few acres of land that he had, with her and her children. Ada would never forget his gesture.   It was no use, though, because after her breakdown she could not find consolation anywhere. What could be a greater time for her than her trip to Poland in 2004 with her fourteen-year old Esse? Ada's mother was trying to make up then for all the lost years. She held and hugged Ada whenever she had a chance. Ada's brothers and sisters were just as affectionate.   Even her nieces and nephews were clinging to her.   Something was missing, though. It was not that same, quiet village that Ada grew up in. Once she was a free spirit there but she could not find herself there again. Indeed, it was still beautiful there but the grass seemed much greener years ago and the mountains more mysterious. The wild flowers were not as colorful anymore and their smell not as wonderful. "Silver shadow" was able to reach Ada on the other continent, too. Ada thought she heard some knocking one night. She was scared but quickly refrained to the prayers. When she woke up the next morning, she found out that something killed one bunny and one chicken in the stable. Was that some kind of the sign for her? Did it have something to do with the knocking she heard at night?

Why one bunny and one chicken? Ada thought. Why was her mind starting to race? She recalled her boss, Onie saying once: "You would have so much more, Ada, if you were not such a chicken". Bunny brought on even worse memories. Years ago she used to recite a poem that she learned as a young girl. It was a symbolic verse, having much broader meaning than the words themselves. Ada found some analogy between those verses and her state of being. She always tried to be everyone's friend, was always willing to help out, and had a smile for everyone. It was just as that little fairy tale went: "One little bunny, enjoying his freedom, was grazing about here and there. And because he was so sweet, playful and funny, he was loved by all animals. Then, one day, as he was grazing, he heard some loud noises of horns and dogs' barking. Petrified, he took to running. He ran and ran until he could no longer do it and the racket was getting closer and closer. He went on begging each animal he passed by to carry him on but no one was willing to help. When all the means of rescue failed, the dogs ate the little bunny amongst his best friends."

Ada always felt that she could have avoided her breakdown if she had at least one helping hand. She tried not to be bitter about it, even though her life changed drastically after that. Every thought of hers was known to everyone, it seemed. Did she pity herself referring to the bunny verses? Did it make things better? Of course not, it made it even worse. People would laugh in her face saying: "It has all to do with a little bunny on the run, or something like that."

For now, she was left alone. She was on another continent with her fourteen-year old daughter. She could not recognize anyone but her own family and very few people in the village remembered her. Ada's mother was very proud of her daughter and she would do anything for her, to please her and Esse. Ada never got so much affection in her life. And Fes could not live without her, too, it seemed. He would call her every day, sometimes even a few times a day. Ada was not used to so much attention and tried to derive it to everyone else. She admired her nieces and nephews. They were all grown up already. Mare had six children, four boys and two girls. They were all as sweet as their father. Esse had a lot of fun with her cousins, not only from Mare's side but also from Acie's and Akin's. They all lived almost next to each other. Acie's oldest daughter was Esse's age. She had a younger brother and two sisters. Little Ausa reminded Esse so much of her niece, Asti! She would not leave Esse alone. Later on, back home, Asti was very angry with Esse for that. She has seen the videos and was jealous of Ausa. Akin's children were adorable as well. She had three, two boys and one girl. Ada sponsored the oldest one, Toi for baptism when she was there in 1992.

Ada was able to meet all of her nieces and nephews and was happy that Esse got to know them as well. Mar lived in the same village, not too far from Ada's mom. She had two daughters, at the time twenty four and twenty two years old. Mar was only one year younger than Ada. Tila lived in the nearby town and she had one boy and one girl. Aria had two boys and one girl. She lived quite far away and had to manage things mostly on her own, just like Ada. Ada loved her brothers and sisters so much. They did not change a bit. They were always together and helping each other.

Ada's mom seemed to be happy, too. She lived in the two-family house that Mare built. Everyone helped him, of course. Ada was delighted to hear about her mother's successful recordings of the folklore singing. She belonged to the group called Kamionczanki. For Ada's mom singing was not only a therapy and entertainment but a lifetime hobby. At seventy four years old she still did not give up her singing completely. Kamionczanki success was attributed to the local council woman and a director of elementary school in Ada's village. The group was performing for some twenty years. It was very successful and made a lot of recordings. Ada thought that it was the best thing that could have happened, not only to her mom but also to the entire village. Folk songs, once so popular at all the social gatherings, now disappeared almost completely. Luckily they were preserved on the albums made by Kamionczanki group. Ada was proud to get one of her mother's albums. It brought memories to her when she was a free spirit, roaming the mountains, with the herds of cattle, and singing the folk songs all day long.

Everyone liked Ada's mom. Fes' sister, Enia took to her like to her own mother. Enia came to Wla's house when Ada was visiting with Esse. They all had such a good time together. It was not the first time for Enia to be in Ada's village. Nearly a decade before, when Ada was vacationing with Anon and Esse, Enia visited there with her husband. Ada could tell that Enia felt quite comfortable and not a bit estranged. Ada recorded everything on the movie camera. She did not realize then how valuable those recordings would be years later. She would get choked up when she watched the video of her maternal grandmother and her most favorite Uncle Anton, Aunt Wla, and even Enia's husband. All those people were gone now. They passed away.

Enia's daughters, Illa and Awe visited Fes and Ada in America. They came only for one week as the tourists. They spent couple of days at Ada's house and the rest of the week at their Aunt Hel's house. Two years later, Illa came to visit again, this time with her mother. Every time Ada had visitors from her home country, she would undergo a mental anguish and anxiety. Enia's and Illa's visit, although very short, was particularly stressful for Ada. She regretted the things she has said to them. She should have never opened up to them. It only made her feel more insecure, anxious, and unstable. Yet, perhaps, the strongest blow to Ada was a week's visit of Kawon family.

Kawons were not related to Ada. They had their own business in Poland and Akin's husband worked for them. Akin asked Ada, if they could use her address, in order to come to America. Supposedly they won a lottery for a resident visa but needed a starting point. Ada could refuse nothing to her little sister. Akin was ten years younger than

Ada and she would always be Ada's sweet, little sister. Soon, Ada discovered that it was much more than a residency address that Kawons needed. Ada ended up signing the sponsorship papers for them, taking the total responsibility for them to be self-dependent, responsible citizens, not a burden on the society. She had to provide the immigration office with letters from prospective employers, for all three of Kawon family members. Ada was still working at Monmouth then. She happened to mention to Zuza about Kawons coming. She referred to them as cousins. Zuza was excited for Ada, it seemed. Mr. Occom had a few businesses and Zuza was helpful in providing prospective employment letters for Kawon family. Ada wanted to make her house presentable. She did a lot of cleaning and bought some new furniture. She furnished the room, designed for the guests, with brand new furniture, including the bed, sleeping sofa, and the carpet. Poor Ada did not know what was in the store for her, in the days to come.

Did Ada get some sort of forewarning that another trial was hanging over her head? What has gotten into Esse the day she asked Ada: "Can you tell me your life story? I would like to hear it." Esse looked different, somehow. Was it really her? Ada told her that it was not the right time yet, and she would not know where to begin. She was startled at Esse's answer. "I know. You have closed the doors and thrown away the keys, but I see it coming back, to haunt you. I see it seeping slowly under the doors." Ada's hair stood up and chills went down her body. Somehow, she knew what was Esse referring to and she knew exactly the meaning of "it". Esse left her so quickly, as if she vanished and Ada was left with her thoughts that her future was pretty grim. How much worse could it get yet? Would she be able to face new trials?

When Kawons where about to come, it rained heavily every day, as if the skies were weeping over Ada's doom. It did not even stop raining when they arrived. Liz wanted to meet Zuza and insisted on visiting Ada at work. Finally, Ada introduced Liz to Zuza but the meeting did not go well at all. They both had too much in common, totally wrapped up in material things. Liz was very disappointed, for she hoped to get a job and make living in America. Two days before their scheduled leave, the sun finally appeared and it stopped raining. Ada took advantage of that to show Kawons the City of New York that was always her pride. They spent one day visiting the city and another day on a boat circling it around. Ada was so stressed out with Kawons visit that it could not escape anyone's attention. Kawons got what they came for, though. They established their permanent residency status.

It seemed to Ada that Kawons brought bad luck on her. Things did not go well at work at all. It was like a conspiracy. Don that always praised Ada for her perseverance and quality of work was not the same man anymore. With each day passing by it was becoming more and more obvious to Ada that it was time for her to leave Monmouth.

Ada was still at Monmouth when another war in the East broke out. She was heartbroken. She always thought the war was the worst calamity on the mankind, besides famine, disease, fires, and great floods. Somehow, Ada felt that everything was her fault. She could never rest in peace anymore. Esse's angelic-like prophecy turned out to be true. Ada became like a ghost from the past, slipping into the future, and having difficulty adjusting to the present. Everyone hated her but it did not matter anymore. Every night she went to sleep she wished that she would not wake up anymore. Yet, when awaken in the morning; she still had the strength to go on. As scared as she was at times, she would still pull through. Sometimes, there were signs, or omens, that almost drove her to her grave but she survived. How could she ever forget that strange thunder storm one day? She was on her way home from work and as she reached her City of Eli, the whole eastern part of the sky was nothing but a ball of flashing lights and thunder. She has never seen anything like it. Ada was scared and started praying. She was even more paranoid, when an odd man, holding an umbrella passed by and shouted at her: "You are going to pay for this!"

Things have changed at Monmouth drastically when Nat passed away. No one there, besides Zuza, knew that she was critically ill. She was a very strong woman and would not let anyone know that she was suffering. Everyone thought that she was on vacation. She was a completely new person, though. When she called the office to ask for something, or give some instructions, she was very sweet and humble. Her voice was so soft and heartwarming. She would never complain, never criticise, or yell. What happened to that demanding and rigorous person? It seemed that in her final days, she wanted to make up for everything, so she would leave this world in peace. When Ada found out about Nat's sickness, shortly before her death, she could not help but to think about the last time she has seen her. She would never notice anything and, yet, that day she saw Nat in her car. In fact, she saw her as vividly as if she came face to face with her. She seemed not to have noticed the car that Nat was driving but only her figure. That was how she would always remember her.

Did Kawons contribute to Ada's misfortune? Soon she would lose her job at Monmouth. She needed the change of environment. She could no longer handle Zuza and her cunning ways. Ada was heartbroken when she let Acil go. Acil was a very good worker and Zuza had no other reason to fire her but envy and fear for her own job security. Zuza put pressures on Ada as well, making it obvious that she wanted her out, too. Ada could no longer hang on, so she quit. She could do multiple tasks at once, at a very fast paced office, but when psychological pressures were applied she would fall apart. Ada vowed to herself that for once she would maintain her sanity and look for another job. Something funny has been going on at Monmouth, anyway, Ada thought. One evening, when she stayed late, some people came to the door asking if that was the place where experiments were being done. Ada was ready to send them away when Zuza appeared and told them to come in. Another time, when Ada worked late at night, she thought that she saw two people in Mr. Occom's all lit up office. She was in her car, in the parking lot in front of the building, when she happened to look up. She was troubled, for she thought she checked all the offices before she set the burglar alarm on.

Days passed by and Ada had a few interviews but they were all employment agencies. Ada was desperate for a job and was even willing to work for an agency, if she had too. Finally, she thought she got a break. Pitiable Ada, she had no idea that each of her moves was monitored, from the time she got up in the morning to the time she left the house for an interview. She was so happy when she received a phone call the very next day after she posted her resume online. She thought it was some kind of the firm because the name was not known to her. It was in the City of New York. Ada thought she could do it. She would not mind to take a train to the City, if she got the job. To take a bus was much easier but more expensive. Ada was scared because she never took a train alone. How would she know where to get off? It was a rainy, freezing day. Ada was waiting by the tracks to catch the train to the City of New York. She was hopeful that the trip would be worthwhile.

Soon, Ada arrived in New York and mixed in with the crowds of people passing by. Everyone was looking funny at her, though. Some passer-bys smirked or grinned at her. It was obvious that she was not welcomed there. She found the place but, to her disappointment, it turned out to be an employment agency. However, Ada did not walk out. She was so thorough completing her application that one of the workers said to her: "It all does not matter". Then, Ada got caught up in a play again. Ever since her first breakdown, she had trouble to keep touch with reality. She would often ask herself: "What is reality?" So, once again, she found herself in a cold, unfriendly world, all alone. Her interview was a disaster. She was completely unprepared to answer the questions asked. She did badly on the test as well, as her anxieties got in the way. Anyway, Ada had a feeling that the interviewer knew everything about her and could not refrain from the occasional chuckle. She felt like there were cameras all over the place and the audience cheered at her misery and downfall. Ada felt so humiliated and hurt that she left the building in the hurry. On her way out, she thought that she has seen someone from Monmouth. His name was Gien, and he was a maintenance director. Perhaps it was someone that looked like him, for the agency was Russian, just like him.

When Ada reached the streets of New York, she finally let go. She was wandering the streets, crying bitterly. Finally, she came to the train station. It took her a long time to find the platform, for the train going to the City of Eli. She was dead inside and afraid to ask questions but she was forced to do it. She sensed the resentment and had to ask the same question a few times before she got a cold, sharp answer. She had a flashback. It was years ago. She was on the beach at the lake. The whole time she could not stop tears coming down her face. She was motionless, almost like a statue. She was horrified, hearing murmurs all around her: "I like the way she cries", or "Good for her". Ada knew for sure that she could find sympathy in no one. She pushed her visions aside, as she stepped onto the train. The conductor reminded her of her brother-in-law, in her homeland, and so did the traffic director, whom she asked to direct her to the right platform. She was so afraid to miss her train stop at her home town that she got off too early, in the north section of Eli. She did not know where she was going at first but finally recognized one of the streets and proceeded home. It took her about an hour to walk home. She was glad that it was dark outside, for no one could see the tears falling down her face. She was cold and hungry; so much for the job hunt.

Ada would not give up on her search for a job, even though she felt that it was to no avail. It was all but a cruel joke, nothing else. Every place she went she encountered the same feeling. She felt like being in the movies, with the exception that she was not a viewer but a player, whether she wanted to be one or not. Esse's predictions came true. Ada's life would never be the same again. Before she would get a break for a year or so but now her mental anguish was constant. There was no escape from it, no place to hide. The evil has found its way to destroy her, slowly and painfully.

Amazingly, Ada got two job offers at the same time. Both jobs were thanks to intercession of two of her former co-workers. As soon as she accepted the first offer, she received a phone call for the second one. The second job was more appealing because it was for an accounting firm, but Ada thought that she should hold her word. Since that day on, Ada thought she made a wrong decision and always regretted it. As soon as she turned down the second job, she found out that her first job was not secure yet. She was called for the second and third interview and, then, early Friday afternoon, before her scheduled start day on Monday, she was called to come down for a background check and a drug test.

As Ada was making her way down to View, once again, her eyes were filled with tears. Did she have the job or not? She wondered. When she reached View, she was paranoid. She had poor sense of direction and felt so lost in that big, ten-story building. Even though Elvi was almost holding her hand, taking her around, Ada was still scared. She did not feel that way before, when she came in for the interview. What has changed since then? Why did she feel like she was being watched? It was almost time for Elvi to leave, so she decided to wait for her. She was afraid to walk alone, for the fear of getting lost. She was also very worried and uncertain whether she had the job or not. After the drug test that she took she was told that she had to take a physical and bring the completed form with her on Monday. Ada was holding her tears back, with all her strength. On her way out, she saw the facility director that interviewed her. He smiled at her and said: "See you on Monday". She felt a little relieved. At least that was some reassurance that she had the job. As soon as Ada got in her car, she broke out in tears. What did she get herself into? She cried all the way home. She stopped at the clinic that she once went to, when she was sick, and asked if she could get her physical for a job. Everyone was very rude, though, and she was told that the doctor could not see her without an appointment.

Ada walked into a couple of other doctor offices. At one, she was told that the doctor stopped practicing and at another, that the office was closed. As Ada walked outside, she thought she heard the evil laughter all around her. She was covered with tears and could not wait to get inside the house, take her medicine and go to sleep. The next morning, when she woke up, she found a private doctor, in the phone book, and went to get her physical done.

So, Ada found herself in a new environment. Was that not what she wanted? That change turned out to be not for the best, though. Ada remembered the day of her first interview. As she was getting ready, Anon let out two black birds that were trapped in the fireplace. The birds were flying around the house, bouncing off the walls, and finally flew outside through the opened door. Were those black birds some kind of an omen, for her not to take that job? Ada worked long, at least twelve-hour shifts, trying to keep her job. Another person was supposed to be helping her, but none of the people hired lasted and she kept on doing all the work by herself. She did not mind that kind of work, though. However, covering the switchboard for an hour was a torture for her. She was so nervous that every part of her body was aching, as she was sitting at that front desk in the lobby. She tried to think of it as her penance but she could not endure it. Finally, she asked the facility director if she could be relieved from that duty. She was willing to assume other responsibilities, instead.

Ada would sit in the four walls of her little, corner office all day long. Sometimes she emerged only to use the bathroom. She was trying to isolate herself from the evil voices around that were ridiculing her. They seemed to know everything that she was doing. When she got stuck, hanged on something, they had a riot. Ada would not give up, though, despite of everything. Her tough life taught her perseverance. Keeping her mind occupied was good for her. It helped her to control her anxiety. She was able to do tedious, time consuming tasks, without getting frustrated. The voices following her track of thinking would not stop her from continuing her work.

When the day was over and Ada got inside her car, then she would let go. She was sobbing every day, on her way home, and even cried herself to sleep. The next day was not any different and so, it continued, day after day. If Ada thought that she had it bad in her little corner office, she was wrong. After about a year and half she was moved to another office. Her job description has changed as well. Voices would often disrupt her concentration on various tasks but she tried hard to push them aside. In her new office, Ada had to interact with residents that came there. Her eyes often filled up with tears when she saw those elderly people trying to preserve their sense of dignity and worthiness. She was always very kind to them. "This is our road of life." She thought. A few times she gently scolded a co-worker, reminding her that someday she, too, would reach that stage of life.

Ada was always compassionate, especially for the weak and sick. There was time in her life that she wanted to change her profession. She thought that keeping the books did not help her in getting better. She did two orientation days for a nursing assistant. However, she discovered it would not change anything. Her traumatic experiences in her life left scars on her. She could not remember the faces and had a big problem of keeping track of patients assigned to her. She could not tell who was who. And when she started training on Hoya lifts, she decided that it, definitely, was not a job for her and never went back again.

When Ada was on a disability years ago, her sister-in-law Hel, asked her if she would mind taking care of an elderly person. She was feeling better already and decided to give it a try. Every morning she would help Mrs. Fran to get washed and dressed. Then, she served her breakfast. She was not a great cook but could make simple things that tasted good.   However, Mrs. Fran usually liked meals prepared her own way so she would instruct Ada how to do it. Ada would then wash the dishes, wipe the kitchen floor, and change the bedding. She would wash the bed sheets and clothes, dust, and vacuum the rooms. She would do anything to make Mrs. Fran happy.   She would even massage Mrs. Fran's feet and give her a manicure and pedicure. She was a little clumsy at that, but did alright.

Mrs. Fran loved to go out. Ada would drive her to the beauty parlor, to the supermarket, or even to grab something to eat. It seemed to her that Mrs. Fran was getting better. It was summertime and Mrs. Fran wanted to buy some new dresses and shorts. Ada gladly took her shopping. She enjoyed watching Mrs. Fran how her face would light up, when she was trying on different clothes in the store. Mrs. Fran's daughter did not like it too much, when she found out about new clothes. Ada thought that Lee was very cruel to her mother, by saying: "Why are you buying all these new clothes, mom? You have a closet full of clothes that you never wear". That made Mrs. Fran very sad and Ada felt bad for her. What "All new clothes?" Ada thought. Mrs. Fran tried dozens of clothes but bought maybe a couple of dresses and Ada bought her, with her own money, two pairs of long shorts. Was that such a big deal?   A few times Ada treated Mrs. Fran to a restaurant.

Mrs. Fran enjoyed it tremendously and was like in a different world. The two of them sat in the restaurant for a long time, talking and laughing. Ada had to leave Mrs. Fran when Acil was about to give birth. Taking care of Mrs. Fran was a very rewarding experience for Ada, though.

Ada brushed off her vision of Mrs. Fran. That was in the past. She was now at View, struggling to keep her sanity and at the same time to do her job. The evil laughter and the phone ringing, with no one on the line but what it seemed like the sound of the life support machine, could surely drive Ada crazy. She hanged on, though, trying to focus only on her job and nothing else. It was not easy to do that. She had to come out of her office from time to time, to do some errands, or even just to make copies. Each time she would open her office door, she would find herself in a different world. It was an agony for her to make it through the second floor hallway to the office downstairs and back to her office.

Occasionally, Ada would run into people she thought she knew. Once she thought she saw her Auntie Sun downstairs in the lobby. She was just sitting there, waiting for someone? Then, on the second floor hallway, she thought she passed by Antoi. Ada used to work with her at Monmouth. Shortly after Antoi was let go, she took sick and passed away. Was it Ada's imagination? Did she really see Antoi or was it just someone that looked exactly like her? Antoi did not grin at Ada, though, and did not send chills through her body. She smiled at her but it was a warm, heartwarming smile. Then, it was Erri. She must have been in her sixties and ready to retire, but she wanted to continue working. Ada would be at the end of the hallway and she would see a beautiful, young lady standing by the office opposite to the copy machine. Was it an angel? Her beauty was almost radiating all around her figure, and she had the warmest ever smile on her face. As Ada came closer, though, she saw nothing else but Erri standing in the same spot.

Ada continued to work long hours and never complained. She was doing at least two people's job for a long time. However, she did whatever she had to, to preserve her job. She knew that if she lost that job, then it would be a very slim chance of finding another one. The economy was in crisis. With unemployment being so high and so many young people with degrees looking for jobs, what were Ada's chances? Anyone reading her resume did not even have to ask for her age. The year she graduated from high school was enough for any employer to take a good guess how old she was. So, she became a prisoner of the four walls of her office. There was no escape, no hope for a change. Everyone tested her and laughed at her. The evil had a good grip of her this time. It seemed that it got her for good. Ada sensed that the whole world watched her sitting by her desk and everything she did on the computer was monitored. Sometimes, when the pressures got the best of her, she could no longer bear it and broke out in tears. She would continue working, with her tearful eyes and her face all wet. She looked so pitiful.

Every night, when Ada left the office, she thought that she heard howling in the staircase, as she was heading downstairs to the garage. What was it, the wind? But the windows were closed and it did not even seem to be windy outside. She could not wait to get inside her car, to rid herself of all the mockery and mind tortures of the day. As much as she tried to hide the tears from her family, it was impossible. It was not any different when Ada's brother, Mare was visiting. He felt so sorry for Ada that he kept encouraging her to look for another job. She tried and went for one interview but could not do it. Something was holding her back, as if she was chained to her job and her office chair.

Despite everything, Ada was thankful that it was she that had a problem, not someone else in her family. She was watching her brother, Mare how comfortable he felt when he was visiting. She could never forget the day she went with Anon to pick him up at the airport. She was hiding from Anon her fears that she would not recognize her brother. However, she hoped that her brother would recognize her and walk up to her. She was getting dizzy, watching the passengers coming out. She was straining her eyes out, trying to spot her brother. There were so many men that looked just like him. They all looked like clones. She was getting anxious and was trying hard to stop the tears that were filling up her eyes. Finally, Mare walked up to her and Anon. She could, then, breathe again. She stayed out from work the next day, to welcome him at her home. However, her mind was playing tricks on her already. When she could not find her brother the next morning, she thought that he disappeared. She was running from room to room, frantically searching for him. Her heart was pounding. What was she going to tell his family back home? What was she going to tell her mother? Finally, he showed up and, somehow, knew what was going on in her head, even though he put it in much nicer words: "Did you think that I went back home"? Ada swallowed her tears. She hugged her brother and made him breakfast. Then, they spent the whole day reminiscing the younger years, when Ada was still at home.

Ada's brother was very self assured and knew exactly what he wanted. "He should have been in America instead of me", Ada thought. "By now, he would have made a little fortune." Mare was very handy with everything, from plumbing to carpentry. Surely, he would have had his own business in USA. And what did Ada have, after all the years of constant struggle? She had nothing to her name but a constant debt that she could never repay. She worked for some thirty three years and, yet, her financial situation was rather grim. She was constantly struggling to pay her bills. Mare also brought back memories from her younger years. She remembered two very popular songs at the time she got engaged to her husband. One of the songs went: "Oh Maria,

Maria-Magdalena you are my Heaven, you are my Earth. ...please always be our hope which we so much long for every day." Then, it went: "Oh Maria, Maria-Magdalena do not go away too far for the day may come that you may want to come back, and just then you will realize that you cannot afford the ticket".

As much as Ada would want to go back to her home country for good, she thought of it as impossible. During the few few times that she went visiting there, she found no consolation. Besides that, she would never leave her children behind. Since she could nowhere find peace on her earthly journey, her only hope was that it would all end with her death. Her brother-in-law questioned her once about her well being. He seemed to know everything about her, as if he could see right through her. Ada's eyes got misty but she overcame her weakness. Her answer may have been a paradox or another source of mockery and laughter but she did not care. She spoke from her heart: "My dear, no one lives forever and sooner or later it will all be over for me. Mother earth with lovingly embrace my weakly human body, for from dust we arose and to dust we shall return".

For the time being, Ada was happy with Mare's presence. He was a lot of fun and liked to talk. Ada learned that when she left for America, her sister Mar continued to take care of the younger sisters and brothers. She was like a second mother to them. Although she was very strict, they often disobeyed her. Two of the stories particularly stuck in Ada's head. In one of them, Mar went to milk the cows and strictly forbade Akin and Tila to go outside, for there was a lot of snow and was very slippery. As soon as Mar left the house, Tila convinced Akin to go outside, to play in the snow. The story went that as soon as they stepped outside, Akin slipped and fell on her hand. She felt a terrible pain and started to cry. Tila put her hand over her mouth and brought her back inside. She, then, told her to go to bed and hide under the feathers-filled comforter. Poor Akin, she wanted to scream from pain but would not dare and only cried silently under the covers. When Mar came back from the stable, she questioned Akin's whereabouts but Tila was able to convince her that Akin was sleeping. Then, Ada's mom came home. Somehow, she sensed that something was wrong. She lifted off the covers from Akin and saw her arm all swelled up like a balloon. Her face was also all red from crying. It was too late at night to bring her to the emergency room. They would have to walk by foot four kilometers to the train station to catch the train. So, Ada's mom soaked a rag in sour milk and wrapped it around Akin's hand. She, then, immobilized her hand, the best she could. Akin's pain eased up a little and she fell asleep. The next day, when she had X-ray done, it showed the fracture and the doctor put a cast on her hand.

To Ada, it looked like Tila was a handful for Mar. Mar would often spank her for disobedience but that did not stop her from getting into trouble. Ada learned from Mare how one day Tila disappeared and was nowhere to be found. Mar was going crazy looking for her. Finally, she started calling out her name. She thought that she heard Tila's voice answering her call. Then, she cried out really loud: "Tila, where are you"? The tiny voice answered: "I am in the well." Mar's hair stood up, and her knees got weak. She was afraid to say another word. She ran to the well and sure enough, Tila was down there, about half way in the well, hanging on to the stones, sticking out from its wall. Mar leaned down and told her to grasp her hand and hold on to it, with all her strength. Slowly, she pulled out her sister from the well. Ada could picture her sister at that moment. She must have been crying with joy that Tila was safe.

As Tila grew older, she was still a handful for her mother, not to mention Mar. She loved hanging out with her teenage friends. There were times when she disobeyed her mother and snuck out the house, with the change of clothes in her bag. On one such night, she got into the accident. She was riding a motorcycle with her friend. As they were passing through a bridge, Tila's friend lost control of the bike. They crashed through the barricade, and fell down the river. It was a miracle that nothing happened to them. They had only a few scratches. Ada's mom always said that it was her deceased husband that was watching over her children.

Tila was a very good student and followed in the footsteps of Mar and Ria to become a licensed nurse. She wanted to come to USA to work. Ada was very happy that, finally, she would have someone from her family by her side. That dream quickly vanished, though, as Tila was denied visa. Yet, she still had her mind set up on the work abroad. She signed a two year contract to go to work in one of the poorest countries on Earth, in Libya. Ada admired Tila for that. It took a lot of courage to do it. She had to master two languages, the native language of that country and English language that all hospital workers used. At least she was not alone, for she had her sister-in-law with her. However, it must have been very hard for Tila because she left her one-year old son behind, in her country. Tila lived in a hut with her sister-in-law. They cleaned and sanitized the entire dwelling, to get rid of the huge cockroaches. They had to watch out for the snakes as well. Tila was a very good nurse and soon was praised by the whole village. After she saved a young boy's life, she was called by the villagers nothing else but the doctor. That young boy was unconscious and no one, not even the doctors, knew what to do. Tila was a very dedicated nurse and she would think of all possibilities to save someone's life. As she looked at that boy dying, she suddenly noticed something on his neck. She was right, that faint blue shadow, peeking from the skin on the boy's neck, was the vein. She quickly stuck the needle in it and hooked up the intravenous. The boy regained consciousness and eventually got well. From that day on, whenever she and her sister-in-law were taking a bus, there was always a seat on it, reserved for her. Even if the bus was packed and all seats were taken, when Tila appeared there was always a gentleman getting up and offering her his seat. For Tila it was a great privilege, for in Arabic countries women were always thought as being inferior to men. However, Tila was no longer considered an average woman. After all, she saved the dying boy's life, outperforming all the doctors that were on the site. That could not escape anyone's attention and the community was grateful for that. She also respected the country's customs and dressed accordingly. Knowing that in Libya, as well as in the rest of Arabic countries women would always wear long dresses, down to the ankles and their arms would always be covered, she did just that. The biggest impression, yet, on the villagers made her Arabic language. She mastered it so well that she had no problem communicating with it. That language was also the way of finding her way out the country, during the political unrest, when all the flights were delayed or even cancelled.

Just as Ada always thought that her deceased father was always around, watching over her, Tila had that same feeling. It was a miracle that she and her friends survived the car accident in the desert of Sahara. The driver lost control of the car, which then overturned and kept rolling down the hill, like a barrel. Where the passengers unconscious, or for how long? No one would ever know. They managed, however, to find their way out from the wreck of the car, and miraculously no one had even one broken bone. Was that not a miracle? Was it not Ada's father's intervention, again, to bring Tila back home unharmed, to her young son? There were many other stories about Tila but Ada got the overall picture. Truly, Tila was a Good Samaritan to that poor African community. She saved many lives and the entire community loved her. It was a tearful goodbye when Tila was leaving back home. Did Tila's accident in the desert leave a scar on her, just as Ada's accidents and breakdowns did? When Ada complained to Tila once, during her visit in the homeland, that she was like a blindfolded woman, for she could not remember the faces, Tila confessed that she had that same problem.

Tila looked exactly like Ada. When Ada left for America, as a teenager, everyone in the village started calling Tila Ada's name. And they had a lot in common, too. They both liked outdoors, where they felt free and in harmony with the whole nature. When Ada was undergoing psychological anguish and came to visit in 1995, her sister Tila was still in Libya. She could never forget how Tila's husband was staring at her. Years later, he told her that he felt like he was seeing a ghost. He took a picture of her and could not get over her resemblance to Tila. Moreover, as Ada would learn from Tila in years to come, Tila's son, Max took her for his mother, when he saw her, and even started running to her, convinced it was she. He even remembers it to this day how disappointed he was to find out that it was not his mother that walked to his house then.

Ada could not help but to think that her sisters chose the right path through this earthly journey. They served other people, helped to ease their pain, even saved lives. There was so much compassion in their work. Mar's work in her home village was very difficult but at the same time very rewarding. She was the community nurse and had to go by foot to attend the sick and give prescribed injections. In her later years, she drove which made her job a little easier. She would often have to make quick decisions, too, even without doctor's orders, in order to save lives. Mar had the ability to quickly assess the situation and take the preventive action. Years ago, there were no cars in her village, and poor Mar must have been exhausted, especially in the winter, when she had to walk in the deep snow and climb the high hills. Her reward was a smile on the patient's face when she stopped his or her pain. Everyone in the village knew and loved her. Once she was like a mother to her younger brothers and sisters and later on, as the nurse, she was like the mother to the entire community. She must have worked over forty years in her profession.

Mar, with her quick decision, saved her mother's life when she suffered a stroke. She saved her life, again, when she was comatose from the sting of a bee. Mar lived close to her mother's house and always kept a close eye on her. She was like a doctor, not only to her mother but to the entire family. Ada always admired her. She wished she could be more like her. Mar never complained or bragged about her work. Everything was so natural about her. It seemed to Ada, that she was a born nurse.

Ada shrugged off all of her memories and thoughts, for she had Mare by her side now. Not that it did her any good. In fact she was more distressed than ever. She did take her brother to New York, despite her emotional stress. They waited for a bus a long time. The first bus passed right by them, even though Ada was signaling with her hand for it to stop. The next bus stopped only because there were other passengers, Ada thought. Why was everyone so rude to her? Was she resented more than ever because she was with her blood relative? Everything indicated that. When the two of them arrived in New York, there were only a few people around. What happened to the City that never slept? Indeed, every time Ada went there before, there were crowds of people everywhere, no matter what time of the day it was. What happened now? Where was everyone? Ada felt very sad and nervous. However, she took her brother site seeing. They took some pictures. She was feeling sick, though, and just wanted to get back home. She hardly managed to find her way to buy the bus tickets. Her brother watched her, as she was going from one information desk to another, walking in circles, as everyone around her laughed. Finally, they boarded the bus back home. Ada pretended that she was resting, with her eyes closed. She had to let out the pressures that built up in her. So, she just sat there, with her head supported by her hands, to hide her tearful face. At home, Ada overheard Mare saying that everyone was playing his sister out when they went to New York.

Mare had visa for six months. He wanted to make himself useful and do some work on Ada's house. It was a very hot summer but that did not stop him from working. She was so worried about him getting a heat stroke, especially when he was finishing up her attic. It was so hot that Ada thought she would pass out when she went there. Her brother had only a fan on, and she found him all covered with sweat and dust, when she came home from work. She did not care how he looked. She went up to him, hugged him and kissed him, asking him to stop working. She felt bad that her brother was working so hard, when he was supposed to be visiting and relaxing. The heat did not seem to bother him, though. In fact, it was making him feel better than ever.

Years ago, Mare had a motorcycle accident and hurt his back. He has been having problems with it ever since. The older he got, the worse his back was hurting him. Somehow, that hot, humid weather in the City of Eli was making Mare feel great and he did not have his pains. Ada would not let Mare work on the weekends, though. She would take him to see some of the famous places, like museums and historic areas. She also took him on a boat that circled the City of New York. There was a beautiful view of the City skyline from it. Ada had little better days with Mare on those trips, even though she could not happen to notice people looking at her, with the smirk on their faces. Mare took a lot of pictures and had nice memories to bring back home.

Mare could not overlook Ada's depressive state, every time she came home from work. There were days that she swore to herself that she would not go back to her job. She would cry herself to sleep but then wake up in the morning to the same dim reality. Who would pay her bills, if she abandoned her job? How would her children feel about it? One thing she knew for sure, she could not embarrass her children or put them in any kind of danger. So, each morning she forced herself to go back to her job. She knew that if she missed a day, it would only be that much harder to go back. Ada was heartbroken, for she knew that each of her moves was monitored and people got a kick out of her misery. She knew she had no friends there. Was there any one in this world that would help poor Ada? Would anyone have the courage to stand up for her? Was there anyone to tell her what was going on? No one seemed to be taking their work seriously. Were all those people around here nothing but actors? Luckily, Ada did not have too much time to think about it. She was always so engrossed in her work that she did not notice anything. Anyway, she did not want to. She would always tell herself: "What I do not see and hear, it does not hurt"

Was Ada oversensitive, or was her work nothing else but a cruel joke? What was poor Ada to do, though? She had to earn money for living. So she hanged on, day after day, forcing herself to get out the house, to enter the flames of Gehena. She was so lonely and cold. She felt like a lost soul. Her only consolation was the vision of "Pieta". That picture stood always before her eyes, when she despaired. The vision of Virgin Mary holding her expired son in her arms, with so much pain in her eyes, was the only consolation for her. Her soul seemed to be almost touching the Holy Mother then and her hands embracing the Holy figure.

Ada's mind adventures led her to madness. She had no control of her thoughts, though, and did not know how to stop it. So, she had no choice but to live with it. The curtain unveiling the past, and her relatives' apparitions continued to torment her. She had no explanation why those things were happening to her, but was her boss Onie kind of cruel calling her a coward? Was she a coward always showing her true self? Was she a coward caring for the well being of her family? Was she a coward trying to stop a network designed to spread the fear around the world? Was she a coward trying to convince the world that God would not destroy His creation? Was she a coward by loving everyone, no matter what the costs were? Was she a coward by being paranoid and therefore, irresponsive to the cries around her? She was insensitive to them, for she could not even help herself.

Ada, who seemed to be so cold and irresponsive to other people's suffering, was in fact very sensitive and willing to help. Her own mental anguish made her compassionate, especially to people who were suffering from emotional and mental disorders. In her mind adventures, she thought she could bring cure to all the suffering. However, her wandering mind led her only to self destruction.

The time came when Ada had to say goodbye to View because she could no longer withstand the mental anguish she was subjected to. She tried to get another job but to no avail. She was not surprised. Who would give her a job in America? Anyway, she came to the conclusion, that none of her jobs were real. Was she just set up in a play? She recalled one of the resident's words once. He was telling her that he has been watching some secret channels on television. He knew, in detail, what was going on in her office. Then, some residents coming to Ada's office were telling her: "You are still the number one". At first, Ada thought they were happy with the job she was doing. Soon, she realized, though, that there was more to it than just a compliment. Ada had a feeling that she has been exposed to the whole world. She was so bitter! All she ever wanted was a real job. She was not a player. She was always serious about everything she was doing, and never acted. And, if the world was dying to watch her, was she not due a decent compensation for it? Should it not the acclaimed saying that nothing comes free apply to her, too?

When Ada sensed tribulations and unrest, she always sought escape in her native country. 2009 was no different than any other ones, but after a week's visit with her family abroad, Ada came back even more anxious than before. It became obvious, that she could not function at all. She felt sick and dizzy. Everything around her was spinning, as if she was on a boat. She forced herself to go to work for a few weeks, only to be drowning deeper and deeper. Ada's co-workers, whom she supervised, turned against her. Did that surprise Ada? Any good that she ever did in her life, came back to haunt her and destroy her. She would not be a disgrace to her children, though, and to all of her relatives in Poland. Anyway, with her mind not functioning, and her depressive state, she would not wait any longer to be told that the company had no use of her, as it happened on all of her previous jobs. She decided to retire. She did not know how she would she manage her financial situation but she had to save herself, for the sake of her family. Housework was a kind of therapy for Ada, but still she could not help her panic attacks.

Did Ada have any regrets leaving View? Yes, she would want to work for her children's sake, but she thought that her office career was over. She finally figured out that no matter where she went, the evil would always reach her. She was done, forever. Did she bring on the bad luck all by herself? She hardly ever talked but when she did, she would always say something about herself. Those little pieces could probably be pasted together by someone, to figure out that she had a problem. So, she could not find peace anywhere. She felt like being in a transparent state, thinking that everyone could read her mind. She started to think in her native, Polish language, in hope that no one could follow her track of thinking. At least, she did not have to deal with her workplace anymore. She could no longer struggle at home and at work. Would the ghosts leave her alone when she was dressed in rags and was all sweaty, doing her household chores? It was summertime, humid, with high temperatures, and her house had no central air. No wonder she has been sweating all day long! She was not left in peace, though. She heard voices outside: "Now, she is a house star". Ada rarely looked at herself in the mirror, but even if she did, she saw nothing else but her plain self and was happy with it. However, did her high school yearbook photo captured more than just plain Ada? Her sister told her once that she looked on it so much like Mona Lisa, on the famous painting from centuries ago.

Did everyone really think of Ada as beautiful? She was so surprised, when her co-worker on her first job said to her: "You must have been the prettiest girl at your school!" Ada had very long eye lashes, that made her green eyes stand out, but other than that, she was just an average girl. She was always humble, and did not allow herself to ever think, that she could be better than anyone else. She was human, though, and at times she could not control her feelings. Every time she went to confession, she would always be sorry that at times she allowed her pride to take control of her. One time, the priest scolded her harshly for that. He told her that she must possess self-confidence and take pride in whatever she was doing. She just could not allow everyone step all over her.

Ada left the confessional crying. She was so confused. Years later, the priest's words were sounding in her ears. She has been so humiliated, that she felt as if everyone was spitting in her face and stepping all over her body. Why would Je want to destory her? Was it not that same Je that seemed to be in love with her? Was it not the same Je that told her once, that to him, she would always be beautiful, even if she came in dressed in a potato sack? That was quite a comparison! Did anyone know what a potato sack looked like? Ada knew, because she was raised on the farm. Could one mistake a potato sack with socks worn on our feet? When Je did his deed to bring Ada down, he laughed: "Not so beautiful anymore. She is real alright." Ada understood the priest's outburst, then, and took his advice. Yes, she was nothing but a nothing, in everyone's eyes but she still had her dignity as the human being. No one could take that away from her. She wished that she could take her grandmother, Stef's advice: "Walk with your shoulders and head up and do not care what anyone else thinks about you." Ada could not walk with her head up, though. She was a lost soul. She could not recognize anyone and wanted to spare herself the additional pain, so she would never look up. She was heartbroken and the sack came to haunt her. When Ada was in a car accident, a co-worker sent her a card. She should have been happy that co-workers remembered her. Yes, remembered, missed not. The card was very troublesome to Ada for the lengthy card turned out to be nothing but a story of wearing clean socks. Reading it, she could not think of anything else but a different "sock", the sack that Je was referring to in 1986 when she worked at AAMH.

Ada's doctor told her once that she intentionally made herself look unattractive. He believed that medication could cure everything and he would give Ada various samples to try, to figure out what worked best for her. He was somewhat right. Medication helped her to control her anxiety but could not bring back Ada that got lost in time and world. She knew that her doctor cared for her a lot. She remembered that one time, at dusk, as she exited his office; he followed her outside, offering a single rose to her. Ada would not accept it, though. She was married and faithful to her husband, even though she no longer was wearing his ring. Fes had to cut it with the pliers, when her finger swelled up and was discolored. Ada did not care about the ring, though. In her way of thinking, the ring was in one's heart. She liked her doctor, however. After all, the medication he prescribed her kept her functional for some ten years. He knew all about her family and, especially, about Fes' drinking problem but never tried to turn her against him. She was sure that he was as happy as she was, when Fes stopped drinking. Dr. Corwin meant no harm picking up the rose from the garden outside and offering it to her. She should not have been afraid accepting it. He was such a kind man and always willing to help. He admired Ada for what she was and that beautiful flower probably reminded him of her. However, the good that he did for Ada was by far outweighing the rose that he offered. Dr. Corwin was sort of disappointed when Ada gave up on her struggle to keep the job and decided to retire. He did not refuse to help her, though.

Medication did not prevent Ada from having hallucinations and panic attacks, though. She could not stop her mind from wandering. She had difficulty to tell what was real and what was unreal. At times, she would suddenly find herself in totally different surroundings. Everything would look different to her, as if she crossed an invisible wall. As she panicked, not recognizing the familiar background, she would slip back to the world familiar to her. It would happen to her anywhere and anytime. Once, she was in the miniature shopping center on Broad Street in Eli. She stopped in the store to buy shoes for Anon. When she left the store, she was totally lost, as if someone rearranged the entire scenery on her. She stopped and looked left and right, trying to figure out where she was. A few people passed by and looked at her with a smile. Soon, the magic spell was broken and she was back in familiar surroundings. Then, when she was working at View, she got lost, driving to work. She found herself in the town completely unknown to her. Was she transferred to Asia? The houses were built in such a peculiar fashion and each of them had some kind of a sign above. The signs were written in the language not known to her. Those were not the letters of the alphabets familiar to her. They were like the riddles to her, or some ancient writing. She panicked. How would she ever find her way home? Home was the magic word; that strange world, so unfamiliar to her disappeared and she started recognizing the streets. For the longest, she was shaken up by that phenomenon she experienced. She could not help, but to think: "Is the life nothing else but a dream? Is the Earth really round and circling around the Sun?"

Besides being delusional, Ada was suffering from panic attacks. Her paranoia was reaching the peak at three o'clock and six o'clock in the afternoon. Ada's co-worker, Elvi once gave Ada a prayer to Jesus on the cross that was to be said at three o'clock in the afternoon. When she was still working, she was petrified to walk out of her office at three o'clock. She avoided it as much as she could but sometimes was forced to leave her office. When she found herself outside of her office, she felt as if she was dying. At home, she would, too, become overwhelmed with anxieties when three o'clock came and she could do nothing else but to pray.

Six o'clock was haunting Ada, too, ever since Esse was about two years old. She was sick one day and had a high temperature. Ada needed to bring her to her pediatrician. She was sick hersef, too. She could not control her anxieties, but it was hard to tell by looking at her, especially that she always had her head down. She appeared normal but if one were to look into her eyes, he would see that they were lifeless. The doctor examined Esse and kept saying that she was the best. On the way to the doctor's office Esse kept saying that she needed to use the bathroom. It was cold and snowy outside, no place for Esse to urinate. So, when they were done with the doctor, Ada remembering Esse's urge to go asked her, if she still had to go to the bathroom. She went with her. The clock struck six and Ada became so frightened! "What just have happened?" She asked herself. Everything seemed to be transformed in the doctor's office. The doctor himself seemed to have aged instantly. He asked Esse to go to play in the waiting room for a little while. When he asked Ada if she needed any help, she started to cry. No one could help her. She would be forever doomed. What could she tell that doctor, that she felt as if she was losing her mind? Was she to tell him that she had a hard time keeping touch with reality or that she did not know whether she was dead or alive? She regretted, ever since then, for not opening up to Dr. Engel. Would he be able to help her, though? She did not think so. She remembered when she was in the hospital for her second nervous breakdown. She thought that she saw Auntie Sun's and Uncle Woo's physician. He was going through Ada's records, it seemed. She recalled him saying: "Now, it is too late for anything". He was right. Ada's breakdowns left permanent scars on her. She would never be the same again. That free-spirit, always smiling, and eager to help others girl would forever be gone. There was no place for her to rest her aching heart and her forever wounded head.

There was something about Esse that troubled Ada. She was only an infant when she suddenly came down with a very high fever. Ada was on a disability then and it was a miracle that she managed not only to take care of her little daughter but also to bring her to the doctor. Dr. Poch was Esse's pediatrician, then. He asked if anyone in the household was sick. Did her depression have anything to do with Esse's sickness? Ada wondered, but kept quiet. What was she supposed to say, that she was mentally ill? Dr. Poch would soon retire but before then, there was, yet, another case with Esse. She came down with a rash. Ada thought it was Roseola, but the doctor said it was some kind of an allergic reaction. Ada did not admit that both she and her husband came down with the rash, too.

Dr. Poch took very good care of Ada's children. He guided her how to nurture them, from infancy to almost adolescence. Ada was sad to see him retire. She saw him only once when he was on his retirement. He was taking a walk around the block. Ada was after her car accident then, and was in the neck collar. Like a robot, she repeated what she was told in the hospital: "Nothing is broken." Dr. Poch looked at her sadly and said: "One needs not to have something broken, to be in a lot of pain". How true that was about Ada!

Dr. Engel was a good doctor as well. Ada alway regretted that she told her psychiatrist, about the six o'clock incident in his office. She thought that when the clock struck six, all children in Dr. Engel's office disappeared. She must have been delusional. What did really happen and what was so obvious to Dr. Engel that Ada was not well?

Ada was not well, indeed, and never would be. Even when she and Fes bought the house, things did not change. She would have panic attacks, when she was home alone. The house across the street came to haunt her too. Was the house occupied by spies monitoring her movements, was it a haunted house, or the dwelling of actors determined to make her life more miserable than it already was? Ada could not step outside her house without being laughed at. She endured it as long as she could. Then, one day the evil laughter and the racket became unbearable. Fes with the children was at the beach that day. Ada took her medication in the morning but it did not seem to be working. She so much wanted to go to sleep, to isolate herself from the "evil" house with its inhabitants. She remembered her doctor saying that she could double the strength of her medicine, if necessary. Ada took another pill and some hours later, yet, another one. She forgot, however, that she could have an adverse reaction to a larger dose of anti-psychotic drugs. She forgot her epileptic-like attacks that she had twice years ago.

So, it happened again. Ada longed for her husband to come home. She could not breathe and her jaws were tightening, crushing her teeth. Finally Fes came home but he was angry with her and was not willing to help. Then, Anon took matters into his own hands. He told Fes: "We have to take mom to the hospital, at once". To Ada's relief, workers in the emergency room were very kind. She was given medication to reverse the reaction and she felt better. She was kept overnight, though. Fes did not stay with her. He left right after she was admitted. Early in the morning, as Ada woke up, she spoke to the doctor, asking him to release her. He had no objections. He knew that Ada was not suicidal and what seemed to be an overdose was not even that. Ada realized that she had medication for that at home. Her doctor has given it to her once for that type of reaction. Ada called Fes to pick her up. She was very happy that she would not miss a day from work. She took a shower, got dressed, and went to work like nothing happened. She heard her co-workers discussing a show. She kept hearing the word "overdose" but tried to ignore it and concentrated herself on things that she had to do. She was then working at Monmouth.

Ada often thought of the visions of her relatives abroad that she encountered in Eli, asking herself if it was possible for her to be transformed and to find herself in her mother's house. Perhaps, it would be possible, if she truly wished for it? She remembered that troublesome day of her first breakdown when Fes kept asking her: "What do you wish for, your family from Poland to be with you? Do you wish to win the lottery, to be rich?" Ada just wished for everyone to be happy and have all the resources that men needed in life. She wished that the good would overcome the evil. Yet, she was once skeptical if the evil really existed and kept asking herself: "Would God allow his creation to be tempted?" However, seeing so much wrongdoing all around her and all over the world, she could not eliminate the existence of evil forces. Years later, someone told Ada: "You have to be careful what you wish for". Indeed Ada's wish opened up a can of worms, it seemed. She would be hated and blamed for all the misfortunes. Nothing was to help her. She had no soul close to her. The young priest from her homeland abandoned her too, just like all other friends that she has ever had. "Quiet waters tear off the river banks", Father Kazi told Fes, referring to Ada. She knew exactly what he meant.

Was Ada to be blamed, too, for all the disasters in the world? Was she to be blamed for all the hardships? She had no control of what has happened to her. Why was she pushed to the very limits? The yoke she was given was much too heavy for her to carry and no one would offer to help. She always wondered. "Was her new world a replica of that left behind? She would never forget the time when she and Fes got lost, while driving to the beach. They stopped to ask directions. Surroundings looked so familiar and the family they came upon looked just like Ada's relatives abroad. There was something about them and Ada would never forget the warm welcome they received. She could not help but to think that she has been dreaming the whole time and when awaken, all her nightmares would be gone.

"What a fool I am", thought Ada when she would panic when the sun stopped shining. "The sun can't always shine. The earth needs the rain, as much as it needs the sun." Fes used to say to her that she would always like to have everything perfectly arranged, like an alphabet on the board. That was true. Ada did not like excitements. She liked monotonous, quiet life. Her mind was like that of a little child's. The verse she learned in her childhood was a perfect description of her imagination: "The rays of sun and heavens all around. That's the drawing of a young boy. He drew it on a piece of paper and endorsed it with a rhyme: Let the sun always shine, let there always be my mama, and let there always be me." Ada would be very much content if the world was just that, she and her children and Fes, of course. Was the world not all but those little segments called families? If all families were at peace, radiating with love and happiness, then all communities and nations would be consumed by it.

Ada could not help thinking that she may have survived on her job yet. He doctor was telling her that her condition was not entirely hopeless. Retirement did help Ada to get better but she was faced with financial difficulty. Esse would always tell her: "Mom, if you will think positive, good things will happen. Never think negative. It's no good for you to be always worried and it does not change anything." She remembered when, long ago, she took her children on a paddle boat in the park. As the children were paddling the boat, they were singing: "Row, row, row your boat gently down the street, merrily, merrily, merrily life is but a dream". Everyone around them was looking at them, smiling. Ada wished that she could feel the same again and sing. Was her life really just a dream? Oh, how much she wished that she would wake up from that dream! How much she would want to be a free spirit again! How much she would want to leave all the nightmares behind her and enjoy her children!

Even though Ada's children were always her pride, she tried not to show it and was always humble about it. She was afraid to talk much about them, fearing that the words would backfire at her, like everything else in her life. However, she could not help but to think that they were the work of a miracle. She could not forget that all the events before her wedding and the nightmare of the wedding itself left scars on Fes, too. Ada did not excite him anymore. They were like two complete strangers, unattractive to each other. Fes asked her to see a family physician. Poor Ada listened to Fes and went, but only to hear what she already knew. What could a doctor do, when there was no spark between two people? Ada was afraid that Fes would leave her, so she went along with whatever he wanted. She went with him to see exotic girls show in the City of New York.

She felt very embarrassed and was closing her eyes. She had to pull Fes out of there, for he was making plans to spend the night there. His curiosity even led him to Goodland. Ada did not want to go, but was pressured by Fes, and gave in to him. However, she refused to get undressed and Fes did not dare to do it alone. They were not allowed to go to the swimming pool in bathing suits, so they just sat there, two clothed people in the Goodland. Did her sacrifice pay off? It very much seemed so. Slowly, Fes recovered from his temporary impotence and it did not take long for Ada to become pregnant.

Despite her sickness, Ada always tried to be there for her children. She did the best that she could. Ada's children always said good things about her. They would bring up the foods she cooked, sandwiches she made them for school, clothes she bought for them, and many other things that she could hardly remember. That was her reward. Her children and grandchildren were the biggest treasure that she could have ever had. They would not even mind, if she went to her native country of Poland, for a few months. Esse and Anon have seen how happy she was there, when they went for a visit in 2009. Her face was glowing with joy.

Ada, indeed, felt wonderful the first couple of days. The long, almost sixteen-hour trip did not seem to bother her. She felt so much at home. She would very much want to stay there forever, if only Acil, Lener, Asti and Fes were there as well. Ada felt so much warmth and peace around her. Yet, she was so afraid of the family re-union! During the sermon in church, she prayed so intensely, that she would be spared an additional distress. She could not bear to be an embarrassment to her mother, her brothers and sisters, and, especially, her children. However, the evil's shadow touched her. She felt its effects already, at the reception; but her prayers were answered, and she survived it. But, when Fes' sister, Enia came to visit, Ada was becoming very sick already. She had the cold symptoms but at the same time the anxieties were taking over her. That same night they were leaving her mother's house to the airport. Ada thought, something was drastically wrong when her brother-in-law was driving them there.

It was a very chilly night. The heat in the car did not seem to be working. Ada took off her coat and covered Anon, who was shivering from cold. Esse was dressed very lightly, too, and Ada was concerned about her. She leaned against her, resting her body on her chest, trying to warm her up with her body. When they finally arrived at the airport, and checked their luggage in, Ada said goodbye to Mare and her brother-in-law. They had a long wait for the plane, but there was no need to trouble Mare and Mar's husband.

Again, Ada was put on trial. As she was sitting in the waiting room, it seemed as every thought of hers was traced, and whether she was willing or not, she was forced to converse with her own conscience. She recalled the night of Fes's car accident and kept whispering: "I underwent my trial then. I cannot endure another one." She was crying bitterly. Her children thought that she cried so much for she was sad leaving her country again. Yes, that was her country once but not anymore, not there or anywhere else.

As they at last boarded the plane, Ada thought that her mental anguish would end. It was not over, though. The plane attendants laughed at her sight: "You should have thought of this before". Ada was petrified because she saw someone that looked exactly like her husband's niece, Illa. Illa came to visit Ada, just a day before they left her mom's house. She made a troublesome statement to Ada: "Do not be disturbed that I look different now, because I changed the color of my hair." Ada kept staring at that person with ash blond hair color. She could not help thinking that it was Illa. She had brown hair color when she came to visit but why was she trying to make it so obvious that she was not blond anymore? Then, Ada could not take her eyes off a gentleman in black clothes, too. Was she mistaking him for Father Stan that once visited her in Eli? That person looked exactly like him and Ada kept staring in his direction, trying to see if he had a white, priest's collar on his neck.

Ada thought she would never make it back home. It seemed to be extremely hot on the airplane and she could not breathe. Her face was covered with cold sweat. She felt dizzy and had a blurred vision. "Hang on", she kept telling herself. "You cannot be a burden on your children; you have to make it back home." As she thought that she was totally losing control and would collapse any minute, she took off her sweater and her shirt. With only her sleeveless undershirt on, she was struggling with herself for the long ten hours on the airplane. When she felt lightheaded, she would put her head down for a few minutes and was rubbing her cheeks and her forehead. She made is safely home and could never be happier to see Fes at the airport. It was a relief that she was home. "Who knows, perhaps that was my last trip?" Ada thought. She was not welcomed there, just as she was not welcomed anywhere in America. She was not imagining that, was she? Yes, her mother would do anything for her. She was there for her, just as she was for all of her children. Yet, Ada sensed a lot of tension and had a feeling that she did not belong there.

So, Ada knew for sure, that her homeland was not a remedy for her. She tried to think of all the good things that she had in life. Fes changed so much over the years. When Ada would look into his eyes, she saw so much compassion. He understood everything now. He was the emotional support for her. He was no longer angry with her for he knew that she could not help her anxiety attacks and if it was not for the medication that kept her going, she would probably be long gone. Ada's children were even more understanding and were always ready to carry her over in their arms. It was worth dying for them, in the literary meaning of it.

As much as Ada would like to wish that her earthly journey would be over, she thought of her children and grandchildren that always gave a meaning to her life. What would her life be without them? Ada could never forget when she went shopping with Esse. She was still working at View then, hanging on to the last string. Esse was looking at the winter coats, and for a moment Ada lost sight of her. She wanted to die right there. She could not imagine the life without her. When Esse reappeared, Ada was crying, but would not let Esse know why. She just gave her a kiss on her forehead. It was so good to have her back. She was always her strength and her wings. She was her dream, her reason to go on. She was her whole world. So were the rest of her children.

Ada would so much want to change things. She would eliminate the Halloween day, and replace it with the Peace Day, or Do Something Positive Day. She would very much want to bring a new meaning to Christmas. Could anyone imagine Christmas without gifts? Yes, Christmas should not be all about gifts. It symbolized rebirth of all nations. She could never forget Christmases long ago that she used to know as a young girl. Christmas Eve was especially joyful. It was a mysterious night. She recalled going to a midnight mass with her family. Outside, the moon was shining, the snow was glistening, and the frost was nose biting. Yes, indeed it was a beautiful night, and the freezing temperatures would not stop anyone from going to church. The church was full of people and the hearts were rejoycing as the beautiful songs and music filled its walls. However, as much as she would disagree with the modern worlds hustle and shopping spree before Christmas, she would not want to disappoint her grandchildren, when they gave her their Christmas wish list.

When Ada retired, she had plenty of time on her hands. She could spend months at her mother's house, if she really wanted. Her children were encouraging her to do so. However, Ada could not see herself away from them and even if she did, the memories from her last trip would prevent her from going. She could never forget the anxiety she felt, when she purchased the tickets. Somehow, she would always feel that her trip contributed to her downfall. She recalled the family re-union. As much as she was excited to see her mother's brother there, she soon was very disappointed. Ada overheard that Uncle Stan had a heart problem but she promised him a dance. She did not know how to dance but could surely move around. Remembering that her uncle was sick she was doing very slow steps, almost in the same place. Her uncle then said to her: "Ada, do not be offended, when I tell you something." Ada asked: "What Uncle Stan, tell me?" He answered: "I have to tell you this, you stink at dancing." Ada finished the dance with him but her eyes were foggy. She held her tears back with all her strength. When the music stopped, she quickly proceeded to her seat. Her nephews, however, would not let her sit down. As if he knew what just have happened, Ada's nephew, Ateu took her dancing and swung her around. Everything was spinning in her eyes. She was out of breath and could hardly keep up with Ateu's steps but did not want to embarrass him. She was relieved when the music stopped. As soon as the music started to play again, her other nephew, Acie asked her for a dance. His steps were even faster than Ateu's but she managed to keep up with him. And then, Anon took her to the dance floor. It was the best dance ever, yet. At the end, he picked her up and carried her from the dance floor to the reception area.

Ada often reminisced her childhood years in Poland. In her mind, she would always have a picture how it used to be, not as it has changed. She would often envision that picturesque view of the hills, with no cars around, but only occasionally horses-pulled wagon. She would feel the cool breeze of the wind, and smelled the aroma of wild flowers. She felt so light and free of all the worries. The old, wooden, brown house of her childhood, with only two rooms and the kitchen, always filled her memory. That house was full of pleasant memories that she treasured. Despite the poverty that the family experienced, there was always so much warmth and love in it.

One day, when Ada closed her eyes, she found herself in her mother's garden, behind the house. She felt the pleasant breeze of the wind, under the tree. The words of the very first poet of Poland would sound in her ears: "My dear guest, do sit under my leaf and get some rest. The rays of the sun won't reach you here, take my word for it. The cool winds from the plains are always blowing here. Here pleasing birds are chirping happily. From my blooming flowers perseverant bees make honey, which then decorates luxurious tables. Apples I do not harvest but my master tenders me, as the most aromatic sprout in Hesperian's Garden." Ada's eyes were getting heavier and heavier. She felt, as if she was enchanted. She fell asleep. She heard a voice whispering to her: "Dream Ada, dream. You have to pick up where you left off. What happened to that picturesque world you longed for? That was your dream, have you forgotten it?" Then, she felt someone putting an arm around her. It was Anon. He said: "Don't worry yourself, mom. You were sick, but everything is alright."

"Mom, wake up. Are you alright? You were murmuring something in your sleep." Ada heard Esse calling and opened up her eyes. She embraced her, and held her tight to her body. She said: "Esse, I had the most wonderful dream. I wish it was true." Esse answered: "Mom, good things happen, when we think positive. Please don't worry yourself. Give me a little more time. I promise you that things will work out."

Ada had a lot of faith in Esse. She would always calm her down. No matter what Ada did, Esse would never criticize her, or scream at her. She had so much patience. "She would make one good doctor someday". Ada thought. Ada could tell Esse everything, without fear that she would ridicule her, or scream at her. She was so unlike Acil. Acil had no patience, and would often overreact. Ada had to be careful what she would tell her. She had to hide her real feelings from her. She could never tell Acil that she was scared because Acil would scream at her: "Scared of what? Tell me mom. What are you scared of?" Ada could never reveal to her what she was scared of. Her fears were unreal, but she had no control of them. Did Acil not see that? If it was not for those devastating feelings, Ada could have probably still preserved her job. However, Acil wanted her mother to be strong, and stop living in her delusional world. Sometimes this worked for Ada. Seeing Acil so strong and sure of herself made her reassured that everything was alright.

At times Ada felt pity for herself. Seeing her grandchildren so self-assured, confident, and happy was making her embarrassed. What was wrong with her? They were just children, and she was a grown woman. Why had she no control of her life? Sometimes, she felt like she was a dice in the game or one of the leaves on the tree that was swayed in all directions. Ada's grandchildren would babysit her. Should it not be another way around? At least, the medication somewhat controlled her panic attacks, and she was able to suppress her feelings. She could not bear to embarrass her grandchildren, especially when they had their friends visiting.

Ada often thought of the conversation with Aunt Fia, at the family re-union. Fia was very devoted to Blessed Mary. She told Ada that for years she was praying the Holy Rosary. She also went on the trips abroad, to visit Holy Mother's shrines. "Trips", Ada thought. She could not help but to think of that white van with "Camping" written on it. Ada was not living in the real world then. Aunt Fia was one of the people that exited the van. Was Ada delusional? Was it just someone that looked like Aunt Fia? Did she see Fia's apparition then, or did she come face to face with Fia and the other pilgrims to Blessed Mary's shrine? There were no shrines in Eli, though. Was Ada transformed to another place, or did the invisible wall open up for her, to see the pilgrimage? Why was Aunt Fia so special to her? Was it Ada's guilty conscience that brought on the apparition? Aunt Fia was brought up in the orphanage. She was afraid of everything. She was very inexperienced, and the unknown was frightening her. Yet, she liked to try new things, including foods. One day, when Ada was cooking 'pierogi', Aunt Fia kept standing by the stove and was annoying Ada. When she, then, took one 'pieróg' from the pot, Ada left her with cooking and went outside. She felt so guilty afterwards. There was no reason to be angry with Aunt Fia. She was an orphan all her life; she was just growing up then, and exploring the unknown. Anyway, at the family re-union, Aunt Fia was telling Ada, that the Holy Rosary was the strongest tool against the evil. Satan was very fearful of it and would not dare to come close to it.

Aunt Fia said that for years she kept the evil away, by praying the Holy Rosary.

As Ada was recollecting her last family re-union, she thought about her cousin Aria. Aria was actually Ada's cousin, Stef's wife. She was not exactly visiting Ada's mom. She and one of the neighbors were asked by Ada's mom to sit the house while the entire family was at the reception. It was a tearful moment when Ada and Aria met. Stef passed away. He was suffering from cancer. Ada learned all about that from her mom. Aria was very happy that Ada, after so many years, would still remember her. She was very grateful for the sympathy card that Ada sent her. Aria had a very long hair, almost to her feet. No one could notice it, though, because she always had it pinned up. Ada thought that in Eli she found Aria's twin. Each time she saw Pau, she thought of Aria. Was it because of her long, feet reaching hair? Pau became a family friend. It was not just her long hair that reminded Ada of Aria. The facial features were somewhat the same too. Pau seemed to be taller than Aria but when she spoke, again the voice seemed to be so familiar. She sounded so much like Aria. Aria mourned her husband's death. She told Ada that she had no spirit of Christmas that year. The house was very empty without him and so was her life. Her children had their own families to take care of and even though they would come to visit, it still was not enough.

"What about Aunt Kun and Aunt Ire?" Ada wondered. She never saw them, since the time she left her homeland as a teenager. She could never forget a letter she received from Aunt Kun, after her father passed away. What was Aunt Kun referring to when she wrote Ada: "About your father's death: I have to tell you something, when we meet face to face." Those words bothered her and she begged Aunt Kun to tell her in the letter. Each time Ada visited her mom, she wished that Aunt Kun would be there. Her words were haunting her, to the point that she asked her sister Mar: "Were you absolutely sure that our father was clinically dead, before you buried him?" Ada remembered that her hair stood up, as she dared to write that sentence. She could not help thinking of the story, told at the table, when she was a young girl. It was about a deceased person, of whom a relative had a dream that he has awaken, and found himself trapped in the coffin. The relative, troubled by the dream, had the coffin dug out and, indeed, there were signs of struggling in the coffin, indicating that he came back to life. Even though he was able to break the top of the coffin, he was unable to remove the soil, and suffocated to death.

Ada met, yet, another of her cousins on her trip to Poland. Aria was not only her cousin, but also her best friend, through the eight years of Elementary School. Aria seemed to be following Ada everywhere. Sometimes, Ada would want to be alone, but Aria would always be there. Later on, Ada would wish she would have Aria by her side, and regretted that sometimes she liked to push her away. As years ago, Ada enjoyed Aria's company, during her visit in Poland. Aria had beautiful children and a nice house that her husband built. She had a rough life, though, because her husband worked abroad. Then, when she started to have problems with her teenage children, she could no longer handle it. She took a heart attack. When Ada met Aria, after a few decades, she thought that she looked good. Indeed, she looked good, for someone that had several heart attacks. Ada could never forget Aria's reaction when she told her she received visa to come to USA. "You will betray our country, by staying there", she said. Throughout Ada's struggle to keep her sanity, she was tormented by those words. She loved her homeland. Was she really a traitor, for leaving Poland and settling in USA? She wanted to help her family in Poland. What good did United States bring to her, though?

Ada often thought that she would have been much better off if she never came to USA. Yes, she did help her family in Poland but, at the same time, she may have contributed to her father's death. She could never forget the letter that her father wrote when she ran away from Auntie Sun and Uncle Woo. His letter was full of grief. He had no idea what was going on with Ada, when he wrote that letter. Ada could imagine what he went through, not knowing for weeks what happened to his daughter. She always thought that grief was the number one killer. Any physical illness is the state of one's mind, she thought. Thus, she felt responsible for her father's sickness and death.

And, there was Ada's mom. She wanted to give a part of her to everyone, not only to her children, but to grandchildren as well. When Ada would close her eyes, she saw her. On that freezing winter night of January 2009, she ran out on the balcony. All she was wearing was just a skirt and a sweater. Ada would always remember her sad look. Was she crying? What was she thinking? Was she thinking what Ada was thinking: when they would see each other again? Was she thinking that they could have spent more time together? Was she thinking if Ada was going to be alright? Was she thinking if that might be the last time for her to see Ada? When the car pulled out, Ada looked back. Her mother was still standing there, wiping off her tears? She had a long time to wait, until Ada arrived home. After nearly the eighteen-hour trip, Ada finally got home, and the first thing that she did, was to call her mother. It was a tearful conversation. Ada's mom had some regrets, that Mare just dropped them off at the airport, and left. Ada had that same feeling at that airport, especially that two young men approached her, wanting to weigh her. They claimed they were taking a survey. That was not how Ada perceived it, though. She felt like she was a cow, being sent to a slaughter house.

Memories of Uncle Woo, weighing her every day, came back to haunt Ada. That was such a cruel joke. Did that joke come back to haunt her in her precious Poland? Her mind was racing. She recalled Auntie Sun's and Uncle Woo's trip to Poland when she was staying at their house. It had to be in 1976. She did not have her legal papers yet to travel with them. Again, they threw a great ball, this time at Ada's parents' home. Ada's heart was breaking when she found out that her parents paid for all the expenses of the party. How could they, thought Ada? How could Auntie Sun and Uncle Woo do that? She sent her hard-earned money to her parents, and wondered how much of it, if not all, they spent to please Auntie Sun and Uncle Woo. The party was so rich, that everyone thought that it was Ada's wedding. Ada's sister, Ria was limping then, because she hurt her knee. Neighbors thought it was Ada, and rumors quickly spread that she came back from USA, handicapped.

While Auntie Sun and Uncle Woo were partying in Ada's village, she was doing all the chores that Uncle Woo left her to do. She scraped all the loose paint on the foundation of the house, and repainted it. Then, she filled all the cracks in the blacktop, in the driveway and in front of the garage. She went to the store and bought ready-to-use asphalt. In the scourging sun and great heat, she was laying the asphalt, on the driveway surface. She was all black, with tar all over her. There she was, all dressed in tar, while, in the third house down, a bride dressed in white was taking pictures with a groom. Did they see Ada? Ada tried not to hear, or see anything. She just wanted to finish the job. She thought she was going to get a heat stroke. She ran into the house, out of breath. She drank and drank, with her hands shaking. Her face looked so red as if she was in fever, or if all her blood rushed into her head. Aunt Ro looked at her, with sorrow. She told her that she should take a break. Ada could not let the tar to get hard, though. She needed to spread it down the driveway, as fast as she could. Auntie Sun and Uncle Woo would not leave Ada alone, so they made her bring Aunt Ro, to stay with her. As Ada looked back at those events, she drew two ironies of life from them. First: her hard-earned money was thrown away on the great ball, for Auntie Sun and Uncle Woo. And second: someone's happiness, like that bride's taking pictures in the garden, versus someone else's misery, like the picture of Ada, all covered in sweat and tar, doing the work well above her strength. Ada would make any other sacrifices for her family, though. They were the only family she had then.

Could Ada ever stop dwelling on her past? Nothing seemed to be indicating that. She recalled the letter she received from her friend Kar. She has been tutoring him before coming to USA. She never knew then, that he was in love with her. Ada was tearful, when she read that he became a priest. Kar wrote that he made that decision, for Ada did not come back. Ada's heart was pounding, as she read: "I know that I will never find a girl like you." Ada would very much want Auntie Sun and Uncle Woo suggest bringing Kar over, but that did not happen. Did that surprise Ada? Uncle Woo wanted Ada all for himself. Marrying her to his nephew would be very convenient for him. Why not, he could have a total control of his nephew. If he would have him wrapped around his fingers, then he could share Ada with him. He misjudged Fes, however, and his plans went down the drain.

Ada was praying that her mental anguish would end soon; she could hardly endure it. She was very bitter about her 2009 trip to her homeland, with Esse and Anon. She could not escape "silver shadow's" touch even there. Did anyone notice what was happening, or was she just delusional? She has seen what she's seen and refused to talk to anyone about it. What about Ada's cousin, Terae? Ada was shaken, when Terae approached her and angrily threw some old photos at her. "Look, look closely Ada, is it really you? Have you been watching too many Reality Shows?" Again, Ada sought escape, in the loving arms of Virgin Mary, whispering: "Holy Mary, Mother of all nations, thou shall not abandon noone, and thou shall not forsake noone. As you held the lifeless body of your beloved son in your arms, with so much despair in your eyes, please pray for us, to end the suffering of our sons and daughters. Your son gave his life for us, and endured so much physical and mental anguish, to bring salvation to all mankind. And you, Holy Mother, what tortures did you go through, seeing your son's suffering! Your suffering was so intense when you stood under the cross that you broke down and cried: "My son please let me die with you." Please have mercy on us all, oh Holy Mother, free us from all the evil and bring us everlasting peace."

Epilogue

As I was envisioning Pieta's scene, I kept calling Jessie's name. She was to get the keys stolen from me. Was it too late? Was the bull already full? I heard it saying: "We are not hungry anymore". Yes, indeed Jessie is fit to wear my shoes. She is so innocent, humble, and sweet and at the same time determined to seek the justice and do only what is right. Caring is her vocation and love is her perfection. What's love got to do with anything? Anything and everything, it has to do with. Love is caring. Love is sharing. Love is faith. Love is trust. Love is goodness. Love is kindness. Love is wisdom. Love is nurturing. Love is cheer. Love is shelter. Love is warmth. Love is patience. Love is confidence. Love is appreciation. Love understands. Love is prosperity. Love knows no envy. Love knows no jealousy. Love knows no anger. Love knows no revenge. Love knows no wars. Love is perfection to infinity. In so many ways, Jessie is just like me, or at least how I used to be. She would do anything for anyone for she sees God's face in every human being. That was I too, before I got my first nervous breakdown in 1984. That girl died then and ended up in the snake pit. What was left of her was the shadow of the human being. In fact, she herself could not tell whether she was dead or alive. Her breakdown followed her like a nightmare and reoccurred every so often: second one in 1986, third in 1990, fourth in 1995, and fifth in 2013. The fifth was her ultimate sacrifice for all of her children and grandchildren.

"My dear beloved: nothing can compare to the trial I had to undergo in the year 2013. I believe it was the fifth and final trial for me, in the form of that nervous breakdown that paralyzed me for almost the entire year. I interpret it all as it was meant for me to undergo the same agony for five times, one for each of my children, for I consider two of my grandchildren as my children as well, for what belongs to my children is mine, too, and by the same token, whatever is mine is my children's. The trials I was forced to undergo have left me 'blind' and 'crippled' so my children are my eyes now, to see what I am not able to see, and are the judges on my behalf, to differentiate between good and bad, or evil. I trust their good judgment as in the midst of my suffering from the breakdown, I heard a voice of the spirit speaking to me: "I know who you are, you are Lottie's daughter. I have heard your cries and came to serve justice. Do not worry yourself with anything for I am always with you. When the time is right, you will know exactly what to say. If it is of any comfort to you, I will bless your children with incredible powers that no one has ever dreamed of. Be at peace now."

I tried to be at peace but the demons would not leave me alone. They were assuming various forms of human beings and found the hospitality in the Cuban household across the street. They monitored my house and watched my every move and captured every word coming out from my mouth. In one simple word, they were putting on an act at their best while I was having a nervous breakdown. I fought them with my whole strength, trying to keep their evil spells away from me and ignored their "mommy" calls. Those Cuban and state demons pretended to be my relatives, or even my children, or anyone I could think of. The biggest kick out the demons seemed to be getting from my Morning Hymns to the Virgin Mary called in Polish "Godzinki Do Najświętszej Marii Panny". The Hymns were in reality a praise of Virgin Mary, in poetry, using many similes and comparisons to anything thought to be beautiful. When I disagreed with some comparisons, I made my own. The Good Spirit praised me for one such clever correction. When the poem compared the Virgin Mary to Abizag, comforting the just David, I thought of it as a biblical paradox. Was it not that same David that desired Abizag so much that he put her husband in the front army to fight the enemy, surely to be killed, so he could marry her? Was that morally just? Not in my eyes, not even if he repented as the Bible had it and scourged himself, to beg God's forgiveness. To avoid that Paradox, I changed the verse from: "You are as Abizag, comforting the just David" to: "You are the eternal love, forever fervent to the mankind". The only comfort that I now find is those brief encounters with the Good Spirit who is promising me that my suffering would soon end. I like conversing in my mind with Him, even though He is sending chills all over my body when I feel Him within me. It never lasts long enough, though, and He always leaves me with unanswered questions. However, when I recall His words from the first encounter that I would know what to do and say when the time is right, I calm down.

"My dear children and grandchildren; do not be afraid of your destiny. It's up to you now to seek the paradise on earth. Nothing is impossible, if one seeks the truth and only the truth. You have been given special talents. Use them wisely and listen to your hearts. May your heart always be your guide! Rid yourself of all the temptations and all mere desires that lead into corruption. May your hearts always be of pure gold and your wisdom as that of Solomon's? Guard the keys bestowed to you. You are meant to be winners. Out of misery, happiness is to be born. Look up to the Holy Mother and let her be your role model. She will always be there for you, to guide you, to carry you when you are weak, to comfort you when you are distressed. She will be your light in the darkness. She will be your hope in dispair. She will be your heaven when you are drowning. She will be your flight in distress. With her help, you will overcome all the obstacles and come out victorious. Nothing is impossible through the Blessed Mary, mother of Jesus, and mother of all nations."

"Jessie, be a role model to all mankind. In the darkness of the night, the light is to be born. Remember that you are not alone, for I will always be with you and pray for you for your guidance and support. I still need to prepare you, my children, for the journey you are to face, for you will soon embrace the Earth, three from the East and two from the West. Nurture the things you learned from me and I pray that your loved ones will support you in all your efforts. You will know when the time is right to let go of me.

Everyone will look up to you, then, like the sailors are looking up to the lighthouse on the bank of the sea. And then, all humanity will praise God in hymns that he finally brought all of his children home. Once expelled from the Garden of Eden and wandering for thousands of years, seeking their way back, will now find His favor."

www.ingramcontent.com/pod-product-compliance
Lightning Source LLC
Chambersburg PA
CBHW060309290526
45789CB00001B/457